THE

CONSTITUTION

YESTERDAY

❦

TODAY

&

TOMORROW

By Barbara Silberdick Feinberg, Ph.D.

SCHOLASTIC INC.

Preface

*B*ecause we've had the Constitution so long, it is easy for us to take it for granted. But we must remember how difficult the Constitution was to get and how it has not been easy to keep. When the Constitutional Convention broke up, someone went to the oldest and wisest delegate, Ben Franklin, and asked, "What have you created here?" And Franklin answered, "A republic, if we can keep it."

The bicentennial of the Constitution offers all Americans an opportunity for a history lesson and a civics lesson, to learn what a remarkable document and system of government we have. It's the greatest story in American history and, in a sense, the greatest story in the history of freedom.

Warren E. Burger,
Chief Justice of the United States, in a
Scholastic interview, June 13, 1986

Barbara Silberdick Feinberg holds a doctorate in political science from Yale University. She has taught in both college and high school and is the author of two books for young adults: *Franklin Roosevelt, Gallant President,* and *Marx and Marxism.*

Editorial Director, Social Studies Text: Carolyn Jackson
Production Editor: Michael Corby
Art Director and Designer: James Sarfati
Photo Researcher: Deborah Thompson

ISBN 0-590-34771-3

COVER: Top: The Constitution in its case at the National Archives Building; bottom: Statue of George Washington in front of Independence Hall, Philadelphia, PA

ILLUSTRATION CREDITS: Frontispiece, Dan Cosgroove • 6, 8, National Archives • 11, The New York Historical Society • 13, Western History Department, Denver Public Library • 14, Leo Casey, 1939 World's Fair • 16, The Historical Society of Pennsylvania • 20, New York Public Library • 21, International Portrait Gallery • 24, Independence National Historical Park • 26, UPI/Bettmann Newsphotos • 31, AP/Wide World Photos • 33, Ewing Galloway • 35, Brown Brothers/Meltyer • 38, Nina Leen, Life Picture Service • 41, 43, Ewing Galloway • 45, 47, AP/Wide World Photos • 49, 52, UPI/Bettmann Newsphotos • 55 (left), Culver Pictures, Inc. • 55 (right), National Portrait Gallery • 57, 58, UPI/Bettmann Newsphotos • 61, AP/Wide World Photos • 62, UPI/Bettmann Newsphotos • 65, Acme Photo • 69, AP/Wide World Photos • 70, Martin A. Levick/Black Star • 72, Culver Pictures Inc. • 75, 79, UPI/Bettmann Newsphotos • 80, Karl H. Schumacher, The White House • 83, AP/Wide World Photos • 85, Ester Bubley for Owl • 86, AP/Wide World Photos • 92, 95, AP/Wide World Photos. Cover by James Sarfati.

TABLE OF CONTENTS

The Constitution on view in the National Archives.

INTRODUCING THE CONSTITUTION OF THE UNITED STATES

I f you visit the National Archives in Washington D.C., you can see the Constitution of the United States. It is carefully pre-served under helium in an airtight display case. The case is designed to protect the document from humidity, air pollution, and vandalism. During the day, visitors can gaze at it. At night, it is locked securely in a vault. The original text, signed by the found-ers of the American government, has survived for 200 years!

The Constitution presents important ideas about how the coun-try should be governed and a set of rules to carry out those ideas. It is remarkable that the document has been preserved all this time. It is even more astonishing that the people of the United States have been willing to be governed by the Constitution for such a long time. During that period, France has accepted and then rejected at least four constitutions. Its fifth constitution is in effect now. Other countries, as well, seem to establish constitutions and replace them very frequently. As a result, the American Constitution is one of the oldest written documents in force in the world.

The word *constitution* refers to a framework, or organization of parts. You may have heard your doctor speak of your body's constitution, the various structures of your body that work together. For example, your mouth, stomach, and intestines work together when you eat an apple. When your doctor speaks of a constitution in this sense, he or she is talking about a system that has grown and developed naturally, according to a genetic plan.

Ancient and Modern Constitutions

In ancient times, philosophers and historians described constitutions from a somewhat medical point of view. They defined a constitution as an arrangement of social and governmental structures that worked together, which they even compared to the organs of the human body. These ancients claimed that constitutions came about naturally, as groups of people found ways to get along with one another. Constitutions were not plans people deliberately invented. Constitutions were believed to grow and develop over a period of decades or even centuries.

Today, Great Britain best illustrates this ancient notion of a constitution. It took a long time for the government of Great Britain to reach its present form. That system of government evolved little by little over a number of centuries without a written plan. The British people do have some famous documents, such as the *Magna Carta* of 1216 and the *Bill of Rights* of 1689. They treat these as part of their constitution. The documents list basic rights and freedoms. But the people won these rights long before they were written down. No one would think to ask the British people and their government to accept and obey rules set down in one written document. Their constitution is better described as a way of life and a way of governing.

The American Constitution is an example of a modern constitution. It is a written document that was prepared as a blueprint for a new government before that government came into being. The blueprint was drawn up more or less all at one time.

The founders first debated the shape a new government should take. Then they wrote down the ideas they had agreed upon. In some cases, they had to invent new ways to do things. They did not have time to wait for people to develop a government gradually. This is why the American Constitution is often contrasted with the ancient idea of a constitution.

James Madison submits the Constitution to George Washington.

Both ancient and modern constitutions are examples of fundamental law. *Fundamental law* is the foundation of all political and legal institutions, much like girders and beams in a building. It creates the basic government structure, or parts, that govern a society. These structures — such as legislatures, executives, and courts — make, enforce, and interpret rules. Fundamental law also describes the ideals of the society, such as freedom and justice. If rulers ignore fundamental law, people lose their liberty. If you start pulling out the girders and beams from a building, can it stand for long?

Both unwritten and written constitutions reflect the belief that governments must be limited by law so that their citizens will be free. This basic belief is referred to as *constitutionalism*. It means that governments must exercise their enormous powers through laws. It also means that there are some things that governments should not be permitted to do. Constitutions require governments to use their powers for the benefit of the people, rather than for the benefit of those who hold office.

For example, constitutional governments cannot put people in prison at will. First, they must pass laws in a certain way, such as by regularly elected legislatures. The laws must state in advance what is legal and what is not. Secondly, constitutional governments may arrest people only when they are accused of breaking laws. Thirdly, trials must follow certain procedures that protect individuals' rights. For example, people accused of a crime have the right to be told why they have been arrested and the right to be tried by a jury. Finally, those found guilty of a crime must receive fair and reasonable punishment. For example, they may not be tortured.

If There Were No U.S. Constitution

Can you imagine what the United States might have been like if no national constitution had been written 200 years ago? America could have remained a loose association of states at odds with each other. Probably there would have been constant squabbling over foreign and domestic policy. This would have brought confusion and weakness.

The former American colonies made their first attempt to avoid these problems when they formed the Articles of Confederation. The Articles set up a way for the states to act together in matters of common interest. They remained in effect from the end of the American Revolution in 1781 to the *ratification*, or acceptance, of the Constitution in 1789.

The Articles of Confederation created a league of 13 friendly states. They sent representatives to a Congress. For the Congress to pass a law, nine states had to consent. Since it was rare when nine states could agree, Congress passed few laws. In addition, the Congress lacked the powers to tax, or to enforce laws, within the member states. As a result, government under the Articles was weak and ineffective.

If the states had not formed a strong national government, citizens of one state might have been treated like foreigners in another state. It is possible that citizens of Massachusetts might have needed passports to travel to South Carolina. They might have had to undergo customs inspection of their luggage and possessions, much as travelers do when they visit a foreign country. Coins used in Pennsylvania might not have been legal in Delaware, since each state might have continued to issue its own money. A pound of meat could have weighed 12 ounces in Maryland and 14 ounces in New York, since each state might determine its own weights and measurements.

There would have been other differences among the states as well. A citizen in Rhode Island might have run for public office without having to take an oath that he was a Christian. Yet, a citizen in Virginia might have had to swear that he was not only a Christian but a Protestant as well. Without a national court system, an act considered criminal in one state might have been legal in another. For example, teaching a black person to read and write might have been a crime under southern laws. Yet it might have been quite acceptable in the North. To whom could a northerner convicted of such a crime in a southern state appeal for justice?

Shays' Rebellion hastened the movement for a strong central government.

Common Problems Unsolved

If each state had developed its own policies, it would have been impossible to collect taxes to pay for cooperative activities. Just think about how difficult it would have been to build interstate highways or a postal system. Or to send astronauts into space. Or to enforce civil rights for minorities. Or to develop nuclear energy.

Under the Articles, each state controlled its own trade and taxes. That arrangement would have stunted the economic and social growth of the country. Instead of acting together, states might have imposed taxes on items made or grown in other states. Assistance to farmers and manufacturers, or aged and retired Americans would have varied greatly from state to state.

Who would protect the public from problems that cross state boundaries? Use of dangerous pesticides, such as DDT, and food additives, such as red dye number two, are just two examples. Protection of natural resources, such as air and water, is another example. Imagine the difficulties of controlling pollution in rivers that cross many state boundaries. Could the several states have agreed on common standards for safe toys and other consumer products?

Easy Prey to Enemies

Even more importantly, could individual states provide for a common defense against enemies? What kind of army could there be if New Hampshire or South Carolina could withdraw its troops? If the American states were not able to cooperate among themselves in mutual defense and foreign policy, they would be too weak to protect their interests. The European nations probably would have carved out new empires in what is now the continental United States.

Under the Articles, the states found it difficult to protect their independence and promote international trade. Despite a 1783 treaty, the British refused to give up their forts in the Northwest Territory. There was little the states could do to kick out the British. In addition, the British declared the West Indies off-limits to Americans. The islands offered a major international market for American farm products. Spain, too, tried to curb the young country's trade. It controlled the mouth of the Mississippi River and refused to give the states free access to the Gulf of Mexico. To sell their crops abroad, midwestern farmers had to pay Spain for passage to the sea. Furthermore, rivalries between the states were hurting trade. For example, Virginia and Maryland could not agree how to share the Potomac River and the Chesapeake Bay.

Under the Articles, many problems arose as pioneers moved west.

As Americans moved westward, disputes between states threatened to become more frequent. Not until 1780 did New York, Virginia, and Connecticut agree to abandon their conflicting claims in Appalachia. (Fortunately, by 1707 the Northwest Ordinance provided rules for the development of new territories that the states accepted so the problem was solved.) With unity so fragile, European powers might have been tempted to divide and conquer the American states. American history might have become the story of many independent, warring states and nations.

In the face of these and other difficulties, Americans resorted to a novel solution. They united under a federal constitution. Until the American Constitution was drafted in 1787, no one had tried to draw up a blueprint for a government and then put it into practice. No one was sure that the experiment would succeed. How surprised the founders of the United States might be if they knew that the system they created would continue to function for more than 200 years.

A pageant at the 1940 World's Fair celebrates the U.S. government.

What has made it possible for a constitution written in an age of horses and carriages to survive in an age of automobiles and space shuttles? How useful is the Constitution today? Is it a brake on modern government? Or is it a sparkplug that speeds it along? Will it last for another 200 years? In the chapters to come, you will explore some answers to these questions. But first, you should understand why the Constitution was written.

CHAPTER ACTIVITIES

Do You Know?

1. Which country has the best example of an ancient constitution? (a) the United States, (b) Great Britain, (c) France.

2. Which country has the oldest existing modern constitution? (a) the United States, (b) Great Britain, (c) France.

3. Which country's government rests upon fundamental law and constitutionalism? (a) the United States, (b) Great Britain, (c) France, (d) all of these.

4. Which of the following actions probably would have been possible under the Articles of Confederation? (a) enactment of a law approved by nine states, (b) selling Georgia cotton in the West Indies, (c) fighting off an attack by a large nation, (d) being tried in Maryland for something that was not a crime in Rhode Island.

For Discussion

1. Do the principles of fundamental law and constitutionalism operate in your school? See how many examples of each you can think of to support your answer.

2. If the Articles of Confederation had remained in effect, how else might the issue of slavery have been resolved?

Research

1. List some modern nations that have written constitutions.

2. Some students might want to obtain a copy of the Articles of Confederation and read parts of it aloud in class.

Playing Roles

Divide the class into two teams. One side should argue why the Articles of Confederation make a good government, and the other side should argue why they do not.

★

A Philadelphia city street during the late 1790's.

DECIDING TO WRITE
A CONSTITUTION

Suppose you are playing softball with a group of friends. Because the lot is small and you don't have enough people for all the positions, you make up some special rules. After a while some of your friends start to argue. Suppose they divided into groups, each insisting that their way of playing was better than any other way? What could you do? Would you insist that the game break up? Would you try to force them to stick to the original rules? Or would you try to get them to agree to a new set of rules?

In 1786, people were growing more and more dissatisfied with the Articles of Confederation. The states began to quarrel among themselves, especially about trade and commerce. They seemed unable to cooperate. So it was decided to hold a meeting at Annapolis, Maryland, to see if the states could settle these differences.

The delegates who came to Annapolis soon realized that the states were divided on many other matters. So they called for a convention to discuss ways of improving the Articles of Confederation. The convention was to be held in Philadelphia in May 1787.

Meeting in Philadelphia

There were 55 delegates to the convention at Philadelphia. Many of them would play important roles in American history. Two would lead the new nation as president.

Presiding over the convention was the Virginian George Washington. He had led American forces during the Revolution and would become the first president. Another Virginian, James Madison, would become the fourth president. At Philadelphia, he took notes about what was said and offered many useful ideas. Pennsylvania's beloved publisher, inventor, scientist, and statesman Benjamin Franklin was there. New York was represented by Alexander Hamilton. Washington would appoint him secretary of the treasury.

Some important Americans were not at the convention, however. John Adams and Thomas Jefferson were abroad representing the Confederation. Adams was its representative to Great Britain. He later became the second president of the United States. Jefferson, who wrote the Declaration of Independence, was America's envoy to France. He became the third president.

No one from the very small state of Rhode Island attended the convention. The Rhode Island legislature suspected that the convention would abandon the Articles of Confederation. They feared it would set up a new national government in its place. A new government might take strong measures to collect the debts that many people were unable to pay. Rhode Islanders feared that the new government would weaken the independent powers of the states and endanger the freedom of citizens. Samuel Adams, John Hancock, Patrick Henry, and other patriots of the American Revolution also failed to show up in Philadelphia. Their views tended to be similar to those of the Rhode Islanders.

There were many differences among the delegates. Some of them were nationalists, favoring a strong central government at the expense of the states. Others preferred to have a central government with very limited powers so that the rights of the states could be preserved. Some delegates came from big states who wanted a greater share in a national government than the small states. Others from small states wanted an equal share in the government with big states. In some of the states, people owned large numbers of slaves. In other states they did not. In some states, people earned their livings mostly from farming. In other states, trade and commerce were the main source of livelihood.

Scrapping the Articles

Despite these differences, the delegates soon concluded that the Articles of Confederation should be scrapped. They proposed to set up a new, stronger government instead. In making this decision, the delegates went beyond their instructions.

According to the Articles of Confederation, the government they set up was permanent. Furthermore, the Articles forbid any changes in the existing government unless the Congress and all 13 state legislatures agreed. The delegates knew that they were violating the Articles of Confederation, but they went ahead with their plans.

Have you ever done more than you were asked to do? Perhaps you wrote a more thorough answer to a question on a test than the teacher requested. Your teacher might praise you for the extra work. On the other hand, the teacher might take points from your score because you did not follow the instructions. This was the kind of dilemma the delegates to Philadelphia faced. Would they be praised for doing more than they were expected to do? Or would they be penalized?

Benjamin Franklin,
at 81, was the oldest delegate to the Convention.

Alexander Hamilton supported a very strong federal government.

The delegates decided to work in secret. The public was not invited. They all agreed not to discuss what they were doing with outsiders. By not taking stands on issues in public, it would be easier for them to change their minds and to compromise where necessary. More importantly, if they worked secretly, the states would not know that they were ignoring their instructions. Then, they would not take steps to break up the meeting.

Similarly, it is much easier to settle an argument with a friend if your other friends don't find out and take sides. Of course, secrets can be harmful as well. For example, two friends may tell you that they plan to go to the movies. They tell you not to tell anyone. What do you do if their worried parents call to ask if you know where they are?

The Preamble

History suggests that the delegates' decision to keep their work a secret was a good one. Later, the delegates explained to the public why they decided to do away with the Articles of Confederation. Their reasons can be found in the preamble, or introduction, to the Constitution:

Thomas Jefferson,
writer of the Declaration of Independence,
was in Europe during the Convention.

We, the people of the United States, in order to form a more perfect Union, establish justice, insure domestic tranquility, provide for the common defense, promote the general welfare, and secure the blessings of liberty to ourselves and our posterity, do ordain and establish this Constitution for the United States of America.

First of all, the preamble suggests that under the Articles of Confederation, there was no common standard of what was right and wrong.

Secondly, the preamble recognizes that the states were having difficulties keeping the peace. In 1786, for example, Daniel Shays and his followers rebelled when Massachusetts courts took over their farms as payment for their debts. The militia had to restore order. Other states worried that they might have to put down uprisings. In Rhode Island, the government was elected by debtors and sought to protect them from losing their property.

Thirdly, the preamble refers to the problems Americans faced in protecting their newly won independence. For example, the British and the Spanish were not willing to let the new nation conduct international trade.

Finally, the preamble pledges the new government to protect freedom then and in the future. The delegates were insisting that they had to create a new system because the old one did not work.

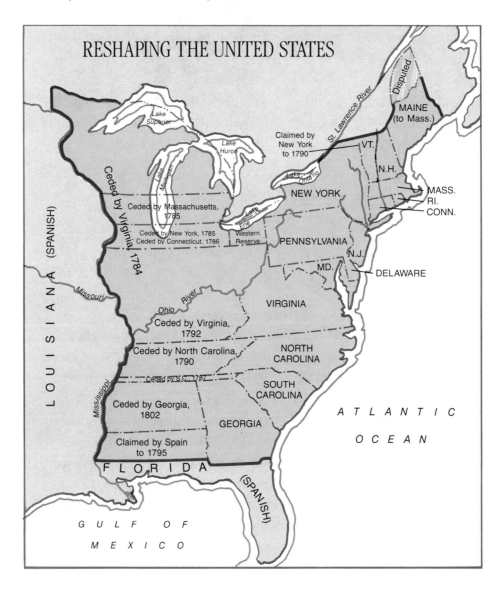

RESHAPING THE UNITED STATES

Lake Superior

Lake Huron

Lake Michigan

Lake Ontario

Lake Erie

St. Lawrence River

Disputed

MAINE (to Mass.)

Claimed by New York to 1790

VT.

N.H.

NEW YORK

MASS.
RI.
CONN.

Ceded by Massachusetts, 1785

Ceded by New York, 1785
Ceded by Connecticut, 1786

Western Reserve

PENNSYLVANIA

N.J.

Ceded by Virginia 1784

MD.

DELAWARE

Missouri

Ohio River

VIRGINIA

Ceded by Virginia, 1792

Ceded by North Carolina, 1790

NORTH CAROLINA

Ceded by S.C. 1787

SOUTH CAROLINA

Mississippi

Ceded by Georgia, 1802

GEORGIA

ATLANTIC OCEAN

Claimed by Spain to 1795

F L O R I D A

(SPANISH)

L O U I S I A N A (SPANISH)

G U L F   O F   M E X I C O

Consent of the Governed

The authors of the American Constitution did not intend to impose a government by force. They wanted to create a government based on *consent*, or approval. They did not want to set up a government that displeased their fellow delegates. What is more important, they wanted to prepare a plan that the states would accept.

The notion of consent was very important to the American people. They had fought a revolution against the British because as colonists, they had never been consulted about laws the British made for them. For example, they objected to the Stamp Act. It made them pay a tax on all printed matter sold in the colonies. This included even newspapers and playing cards. Colonists were not represented in Parliament, the British legislature. The famous slogan "No taxation without representation" expressed their anger at being denied a say in how they were governed.

This is why the delegates were so determined to agree on the Constitution they were writing. They knew that the new government would succeed only if it were acceptable to the states. If the states did not consent to the Constitution, they would not put it into effect. If they agreed to it, they would pledge their cooperation. Thus the delegates insisted that the Constitution could not go into effect until it had been *ratified*, or approved, by at least nine of the 13 original states.

How were the delegates going to get the states to consent? How could they make the new system appeal to so many different and conflicting interests? A lot would depend on the compromises they could achieve among themselves. Even more would depend on the ideas about government that the Constitution proposed. In the end, those ideas and the ways they were to be carried out would justify what the delegates to Philadelphia did.

The delegates sign the Constitution, September 1787.

CHAPTER ACTIVITIES

Do You Know?

1. Where did the delegates meet to write the U.S. Constitution? (a) Annapolis, (b) Philadelphia, (c) Washington.

2. Which of the following famous Americans attended the convention? (a) George Washington, (b) James Madison, (c) Thomas Jefferson, (d) Benjamin Franklin.

3. Which of the following does the preamble say are the reasons for writing a constitution? (a) to end tyranny, (b) to form a better union, (c) to provide protection for everyone, (d) to give everyone a better life, (e) to make trade easier.

4. What does the slogan "No taxation without representation" mean? (a) People should not have to pay high taxes. (b) People should be able to vote for the taxes they pay. (c) Taxes should represent the amount of wealth a nation has.

For Discussion

1. Do you think the delegates' idea not to meet in public was a good one? Explain. When, if ever, do you think public officials should meet in private today?

2. Why was it so important for the states to consent to the new plan? How important is consent today to governing the United States?

Research

1. Read the Preamble to the Constitution in your text and then use a dictionary to find out the meaning of the following words: *tranquility, posterity,* and *ordain.*

2. From the Constitution at the back of your book, find out the qualifications for representative, senator, and president.

Playing Roles

Some students might take the parts of Samuel Adams, John Hancock, and Patrick Henry in telling why they opposed the meeting in Philadelphia.

3

Currency of the young republic.

DEVELOPING GUIDELINES

How were the delegates to form "a more perfect union"? Suppose you and a group of your friends are hiking in a wilderness. A few of you get separated from the main party and your leaders. How would you fend for yourselves until you were found? Waiting for help could be difficult if each person had a different idea about what to do. How would you decide where to seek shelter? How would you divide chores? What if some people wanted to gather firewood, and no one wanted to stand watch? Would it make sense to find out where everyone agreed and start out from there? Would it be wise to talk over your differences and try to reach a series of compromises? This is the approach the founders of the American government took.

The delegates to the constitutional convention shared some ideas. They also disagreed about the best way to carry out those ideas. For this reason they held lengthy discussions to work out compromises. They all wanted a *republican* form of government. That is, they wanted a government run by elected officials rather than one ruled by a queen or king. After fighting to gain independence from the British government of King George III, they did not want another monarchy.

A republic of associated states had proved ineffective under the Articles of Confederation. Alexander Hamilton proposed doing away with the states and forming one vast national government. But the other delegates were not about to agree to this. Most people still thought of themselves more as citizens of their states, as Rhode Islanders or Georgians, than as Americans. Rhode Islanders, in fact, had feared such a plan. That's why they had not sent a delegate. The delegates had to find some way to avoid the weaknesses of their present government without absorbing the states.

A Federal Republic

The solution was *federalism*. With federalism, people are citizens of both the nation and of the state in which they live. To make federalism work, some of the laws they obey are national laws, some are state laws, and some are shared. That is, they are both national and state laws.

The making and control of money is an example of a purely national task. Nickels, dimes, and other coins can be made only by national government. States may not make or regulate money.

Laws governing the use of seat belts are examples of purely state business. If you ride in a car in New York, state law requires you to wear a seat belt. In other states, you may not have to — legally.

In other matters, the state and national governments share

power. For example, both state and national governments tax your family's long distance telephone bill. If a state law conflicts with a national law, the national law dominates.

The delegates in Philadelphia were determined to replace the confederation with a strong national government. But they were also concerned lest the national government become too powerful. They wanted the rights of the citizens and each state to be protected. In the doctrine of *separation of powers*, they found a solution to their dilemma.

The authors set apart the legislative (law-making), executive (law-enforcing), and judicial (law-interpreting) powers of the national government. The Congress, made up of the Senate and the House of Representatives, is the legislative branch. The president leads the executive branch. The court system is the judicial branch. Each has different functions.

To understand how this works, imagine sharing a cupcake with a friend. If you divide the cupcake and take your share, might your friend complain that you got the larger part? If your friend splits the cupcake and takes a share, wouldn't you be tempted to com-

THE THREE BRANCHES

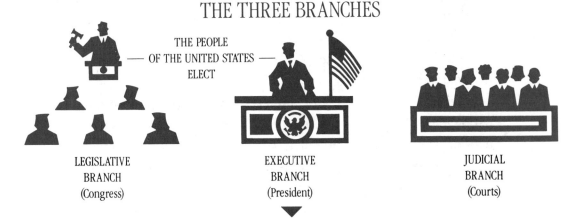

THE PEOPLE
— OF THE UNITED STATES —
ELECT

LEGISLATIVE
BRANCH
(Congress)

EXECUTIVE
BRANCH
(President)

JUDICIAL
BRANCH
(Courts)

EXECUTIVE DEPARTMENTS

plain about your portion? If however, one persons slices, and the other selects the portion he or she wants, the results are more likely to be fair. With separation of powers, in a sense, one group does the dividing and another group chooses. Power is not concentrated in one person or group. It is split up in order to achieve a common goal.

Checks and Balances

To make sure that officeholders would not abuse their powers, the founders put into practice the doctrine of *checks and balances.* Each branch tries to make sure that the other branches are not becoming too powerful at its expense. The rivalry among the branches keeps them from joining together to deprive citizens of their liberty.

To see what the founders had in mind, suppose that you and a group of classmates are assigned a project. To begin, you divide the tasks. You might argue about who is to do what. One of you might collect information. Another might write down what you learn. A third might make the drawings. As you work, each of you probably contributes to the others' work by criticizing and by suggesting improvements. You are, in effect, interfering in each other's work. As you cooperate to complete the assignment, each of you may also be competing.

In the national government, checks and balances combine competition and cooperation. For example, the president appoints the justices of the Supreme Court. The Senate must approve of those appointments, however. Members of the Supreme Court may be asked to decide if decisions made by the president or the Congress violate the principles of the Constitution. However, under certain circumstances, Congress can remove members of the Supreme Court from office.

Sometimes controversy arises over presidential appointments to the Supreme Court. In the late 1960's and early 1970's, the Senate turned down President Nixon's nominations of Clement Haynesworth, Jr. and later G. Harrold Carswell. Senators felt that these nominees might not decide questions about race impartially because they had poor records on civil rights issues. The Senate did approve Nixon's appointment of Chief Justice Warren Burger and Harry A. Blackmun as Associate Justice of the Supreme Court. More recently, the Senate approved President Reagan's nomination of Sandra Day O'Connor. In September 1986, the Senate also approved President Reagan's nominations of Antonin Scalia as Associate Justice, and Justice William Rehnquist to Chief Justice Burger's seat when he retired.

Representative Democracy

The Constitution's authors believed in *representative democracy*. That is government by individuals regularly elected by the people. Members of the colonial legislatures, and later, the state legislatures, had been elected by people. So the delegates agreed that voters should elect the members of the new national government. However, they could not agree on who should vote and how many government officials should be elected directly. They also debated how voting *within* the national government should take place.

Who Should Vote

In the 18th century, few people were concerned with letting women or minorities, such as free blacks, vote. Instead, the delegates argued about whether every white man should vote, or only those who owned property. Some delegates believed that all white men should vote because they were the best judges of who was fit

Sandra Day O'Connor, the first woman to be appointed to the Supreme Court, and Chief Justice Warren Burger.

to govern thcm and who was not. For example, they knew how much they could buy when prices went up or down. As fathers, husbands, and sons, they knew what it meant to go off to war.

Other delegates did not trust the judgment of ordinary men. They felt that the average man was too uninformed to vote for many government officials. In addition, they were concerned that the many farmers and workers would support candidates who would cancel their debts. Shays' Rebellion was still fresh in these delegates' minds. They were very distrustful of Americans who lacked property or wealth.

Since the issue was difficult to resolve, the matter was left for the states to settle. Some states set stiff requirements about the amount of land that voters had to own. This limited the number of men who could vote. Other states were more lenient. However, as people began to move westward, they found acres and acres of land waiting to be settled. Then the issue of property became less important. By the 1830's, most states agreed that all white men over 21 were qualified to vote whether or not they owned land.

Electing the President

The delegates in Philadelphia were divided over how many officials should be elected directly. Some of the delegates wanted voters to choose all members of the national government. They argued that if the government was to serve the interests of the nation, it had to be chosen directly by the people and held directly responsible to them. Otherwise the officials might be tempted to use their powers to benefit themselves, not the public.

Other delegates preferred to limit the voters' choices. These founders feared tyranny of the majority. By that they meant the possibility that a large group of voters would take control of the new government for selfish purposes rather than for the good of the nation. If the majority could vote for all members of the national government, they would control it. The delegates were afraid that the poorer, less informed Americans would form just such a large group, able to make the government do what it wanted. This may be why the delegates argued that a majority is not always right because it is more numerous than a minority.

Suppose after a test you compare your answers to those of your friends. How would you feel if your answer to a key question is different from all of theirs? How would you feel if they insisted that your answer was wrong? What if it later turned out that your an-

Voters await their turn at the polls on Election Day, 1932.

swer was correct? Would you then want the correct answer to be decided by majority vote?

Some of the founders did not trust the judgment of the majority of their fellow citizens. Others did, so the delegates compromised on this issue. Under the original Constitution only the House of Representatives was directly elected. All other offices of the national government were indirectly elected. Voters elected state legislators who in turn chose the Senate. The president was elected through a very complicated process known as the *electoral college.*

Electoral College

Under this system, people in every state vote for the president. The candidate with the most votes wins *all* the state's electoral votes. The losing candidate receives no electoral votes, no matter how close the election is. The electoral votes are cast by special delegates called electors. The number of electors in each state is based on the state's population. Larger states have more electors. Together, the electors form the electoral college. Their votes actually choose the president.

The candidate with a majority of electoral votes becomes president. If no candidate achieves a majority, the election goes into the House of Representatives. There each state has one vote. Thus, the method for electing the president is a compromise between those who favored direct election and those who did not.

Setting Terms

To make it even harder for a majority to control the national government, the founders staggered the terms of elected officials. Members of the House of Representatives serve two years. Senators serve for six years, but one-third of the Senate faces the voters every two years. Presidents serve four-year terms.

In addition, different *electorates,* groups of voters, choose these national officials. Representatives were elected by voters in local districts, senators by state legislatures, and the president by all the voters and by electors. This ensured that it would be difficult for a majority to control the national government.

Voting within the Government

The delegates also debated about voting within the national government. The small states wanted a voice equal to big states. Under the Articles, each state, regardless of its size, had one vote in Congress. States with large populations felt that they were underrepresented because small states had the same voice.

Again, the founders compromised. They decided that the small states would be equal partners of the big states in the Senate. In the House of Representatives, the large states would have an advantage over the small states. In the Senate, each state would have two votes, one for each senator. In the House of Representatives, a state's population would determine its number of representatives. Together, the Senate and the House would be known as Congress.

Slaves pick cotton while an overseer on horseback watches.

Slavery Considered

The founders also compromised on the issue of slavery. Slaves were much more numerous in the agricultural South than the industrial North. The founders decided that slaves would be counted as three-fifths of a free person for purposes of taxation and representation. The northern states did not want southern states to have more representatives in Congress because there were more slaves in the South. The southern states did not want to pay more taxes because they had more slaves, therefore more people. The Constitution also put a limit on bringing in slaves from abroad. It declared that slave trade must end in 1808.

The Constitution put into practice the ideas of republicanism, federalism, separation of powers, checks and balances, and representative democracy. Delegates negotiated compromises so that these ideas would reflect the interests of citizens from big states and small states, the propertied and the debtors, the North and the South. Today these ideas continue to be adapted to the changing needs of the people. Perhaps one reason why the Constitution is still in effect is that Americans still believe in most of the ideas it contains.

CHAPTER ACTIVITIES

Do You Know?

1. Which of the following governments were republics? (a) the American government under the Articles of Confederation, (b) the American government under the federal Constitution, (c) the British government.

2. What best describes the government proposed by Alexander Hamilton? (a) a monarchy, (b) an all-powerful national government, (c) a confederation.

3. In which of the following activities do the states and the federal government share power? (a) minting coins, (b) collecting taxes on gasoline, (c) setting qualifications for voting.

4. Which of the following are examples of separation of powers? (a) Congress passes laws. (b) The President is commander-in-chief of the army. (c) Supreme Court Justices are nominated by the President.

5. Which of the following are examples of checks and balances? (a) The Senate must confirm the President's nominations to the Supreme Court. (b) The Supreme Court overrules a law passed by Congress. (c) Congress sets standard weights and measures.

For Discussion

1. Do you think the idea of tyranny of the majority should be of concern today? Give reasons for your answer.

2. How has the election of senators changed since the Constitution was written? Why do you think this change was made?

3. Do you think the electoral college is a good idea for modern times? Explain your answer.

Research

1. Look up Article 1, Section 6 of the Constitution. How does it relate to the principle of separation of powers?

2. The principles of separation of powers and checks and balances come from the English philosopher John Locke and the French philosopher Baron de Montesquieu. Find out more about them.

Playing Roles

Students in the roles of slaves, women, Rhode Islanders, and a future candidate for president might give speeches for or against the election system described in the Constitution.

★

SORTING OUT RELATIONSHIPS

I f you were to set down all the rules affecting relationships in your family, how would you do it? Would you mention all the things you expect your parents to do for you and all the things they expect you to do? Would you describe the way you should treat your brothers and sisters? Would you want to include the way they should treat you and your property?

You might find it very difficult to draw up such a list. If you wrote down everything in great detail, such as week-night bedtimes, you might find the list too limiting. What if something happened that was not covered by your list, such as a school play that ran late? What would happen when you were older? Would you still have to go to bed at your old bedtime?

On the other hand, if you just put in a few general statements, such as going to bed at a "reasonable hour," you might also run into difficulties. Who could decide what "reasonable" meant? Or suppose you wrote a statement saying that you would respect your sisters' and brothers' privacy and they would respect yours. Who would interpret what the right to privacy included? Suppose the telephone was in the same room in which your brother was watching a television program when you received a call. Would your right to privacy come before his right to watch his program? What would you do if you needed to call a friend to get a home-work assignment and your sister was on the phone? Could you interrupt her conversation?

Rules describing relationships can be very complicated. The authors of the Constitution had to sort out many relationships. There were those among the states, between the states and the national government, among branches of the national government, and between the governments and the people. What a difficult task they faced!

Relationships Among States

The founders expected that the states would settle their quar-rels without resorting to force. The states are required to negoti-ate agreements among themselves or to take their disagreements to a federal court.

Under an *extradition* requirement, states are asked to return criminals who have fled from a state in which they face trial or imprisonment. During the 1850's this created a problem for north-ern states who did not want to return runaway slaves to their masters in the South. They did not think this requirement was fair.

The states must also give *full faith and credit* to each others' official acts. Full faith and credit means that, for example, if you were born in New Jersey, other states would recognize your birth certificate as proof of your age. Each state is required to honor the public documents and records of the other states.

States must offer the *privileges and immunities* of their citizens to citizens of other states. This means that if you live in New Hampshire and visit California, you do not have to pay a special visitors' tax on things you buy there. As a visitor, you have the same civil rights as citizens of California. For example, you can get a job or rent an apartment. But you do not have the same political rights. For instance, you can't vote or serve on a jury, because you do not live there permanently.

National Obligations to States

The Constitution requires the national government to guarantee the states a *republican form of government.* The delegates did not define exactly what they meant by this phrase. But if a state suddenly became a monarchy or a dictatorship, Congress could enforce this guarantee.

The national government must also protect states from *domestic insurrection.* If there is an uprising or riot in a state, state officials may request that the president send troops to help them keep the peace. In 1849, Rhode Island's government was challenged by a rival government. President John Tyler threatened to send in troops to support the existing government. That government stayed in power.

The national government may admit new states to the union. However, it may not form a new state out of territory belonging to another state without that state's consent. For example, the state of Kentucky was formed in 1792 from land that had belonged to Virginia.

The national government may not tax *exports.* These are items produced for sale abroad. This rule was especially important to southern states which sent crops such as cotton to Europe. An export tax would have forced them to raise their prices. Thus they would have found fewer foreign buyers. This constitutional restriction helped manufacturers when the United States became an industrial nation. For a long time, it helped Americans sell their products to foreign buyers.

Dockworkers on the Hudson River waterfront unload a ship's cargo.

National Powers

The Constitution gives the national government certain exclusive powers that belonged to the states under the Articles. As a result, only the national government may

- make treaties with foreign governments,

- declare war,

- set aside parts of legal agreements,

- mint money, or

- collect fees on *imports.* These are items brought into the United States for sale.

Only the national government may regulate *interstate commerce.* The national government sets up rules affecting products whose parts are manufactured in more than one state or nation and which are sold across state or national lines. Cars and TV sets are often made this way. This prevents states from setting up trade barriers by placing extra taxes on things produced out of state.

States kept the power to regulate *intrastate commerce,* trade within their boundaries. For example, the national government has no control over orange juice grown, packaged, and sold in Florida. If you live in Florida and buy a carton of this orange juice, you are involved in intrastate commerce. How can you be certain that you are drinking pure Florida orange juice? If there is no label to tell you so, the juice may be made from oranges picked in California and processed in Texas. It might be even be packaged in Georgia. Then your carton of juice would serve as an example of interstate commerce.

A truck carries goods across the Rocky Mountains.

Shared Powers

The states and the national government also share certain powers. For example, states can set speed limits for trains in crowded cities. However, since national laws affect citizens of every state, the Constitution makes national law more powerful than state law if the two conflict.

The nation and the states share control over national elections. The states may set the time for an election to take place, such as between 8 A.M. and 9 P.M. They may choose polling places, such as schools. They may also determine voting methods, such as whether voting machines will be used. Congress has the right to change the state regulations, however.

Sharing powers encourages states to experiment with laws that the nation may later adopt. For example, in the early 1900's many states banned child labor. This prevented many young children from working long hours in factories. The national government was unsuccessful in its attempts to pass a similar law. When state laws required children to attend elementary and high school, child labor became less common. Sharing power also allows the states to handle problems, such as raising money for education by taxes and lotteries.

Powers Divided Among the Branches

The idea of shared and exclusive powers also affects the relationship between the three branches of the national government. The Constitution discusses what members of each branch of government may or may not do. It also lists the qualifications they must have, such as the youngest age at which they may hold office. It describes the way they must perform their separate and shared functions. With some adjustments, these rules still govern the way the president, the legislature, and the courts work. The relationships among the branches of government can be quite complicated.

Presidential powers. According to the Constitution, the president is the commander-in-chief of the armed services. But Congress has the right to declare war as well as to make rules and grant funds for the armed forces. The president has responsibility for foreign affairs. He or she may sign treaties and appoint ambassadors, but the Senate must approve these decisions.

As chief executive, the president must see that the laws are carried out, but Congress provides funds for this. The Senate must approve the appointments of department heads and other high federal officials as well as federal judges. Only the president may

*Federal troops escort nine black students into
an all-white school in Little Rock, Arkansas in 1957.*

call Congress into special session. If the two houses disagree on a closing date, she or he has the authority to decide when their sessions will end.

Congressional powers. The law-making process demonstrates that sharing separated powers is not simple. The Congress has the sole right to make laws. Congress alone may raise taxes and borrow money. All money bills must first be proposed in the House of Representatives. That is because only representatives were directly elected at first. Yet the president may address Congress to suggest new laws, including laws to raise and lower taxes.

More importantly, the president has the right to *veto* laws made by Congress, to set them aside or disapprove of them. Most of the time, if a president vetoes a law, it must return it to Congress. Then, Congress can pass the law again, this time by a two-thirds vote. This is known as *overriding* the president's veto.

Only Congress can set rules for the way

- immigrants become citizens (naturalization),
- businesses and individuals make arrangements for debts they cannot repay (bankruptcy), and
- inventors and artists protect their work (patents and copyrights).

Because common standards are needed, Congress controls the coinage, sets weights and measures, and regulates the postal service. In addition, Congress was given the power to govern the District of Columbia.

Congress also has the power to set up a national court system. Under this power, Congress set up federal district courts to try cases and circuit courts to hear appeals.

Judicial powers. The Constitution sets up federal courts, including the Supreme Court. These courts hear cases involving federal laws, the Constitution itself, as well as treaties and the law of the seas. Controversies between states, between citizens of different states, and cases involving foreign ambassadors to the United States are among the types of cases that were originally to be tried in federal courts. This list shows that the founders expected the courts to sort out the tangle of relationships that would result from the government they created.

Federal courts also try cases involving *treason.* The Constitution defines treason very carefully. Treason is the waging of war against the United States or siding with and helping its enemies. It is important to distinguish treason from loyal opposition to the government. Otherwise, government officials might charge rival politicians with treason. The Constitution also describes the procedures the courts must follow in order to convict a person of treason. The punishment, though, is to be decided by Congress.

The president, vice president and other high officials can be removed from office for treason. The Constitution also mentions high crimes or misdemeanors as grounds for removal. In this case Congress exercises judicial power. The House of Representatives starts inquiries, known as *impeachment,* to see if there is a reason to remove the person from office. Then the Senate holds a trial to decide if the official is innocent or guilty.

In 1974, the House began to look into charges that President Nixon should be impeached. He was accused of trying to prevent the courts from finding out whether the committee heading his campaign for reelection broke laws against bribery and corruption. President Nixon chose to resign before the House could vote on the charges. Gerald Ford, his successor, granted him a full pardon. It excused Nixon of any offenses he might have committed during his presidency. According to the Constitution, the chief executive may pardon any misconduct except impeachment. Of course, Nixon was never impeached.

The Senate Watergate investigating committee hears testimony involving President Nixon in 1973.

In their relations with citizens, both the states and the national government may use only those powers given to them in the Constitution. The authors tried to provide further guarantees to protect the liberty of the American people. They added specific limits on governments. They did this to discourage officials from abusing their powers.

Limits on Government

The Constitution forbids state and national governments from granting titles of nobility. In Great Britain and most European nations, noble titles were passed from parent to child. This created a class of privileged people. The founders feared that such a noble class would destroy representative democracy in America. Some people would have more rights by birth than others.

The founders also made certain that American legislatures would not abuse their powers as the British Parliament had from time to time. They would not let Congress or the state legislatures pass laws that punished specific people or groups without a trial. Neither would they let legislatures pass laws punishing acts that were legal at the time they were committed. They forbid the national government the power to suspend the writ of habeas corpus except in times of rebellion or invasion.

Laws which punish specific individuals or groups without benefit of a trial are called *bills of attainder.* The Constitution prohibits them. In 1943, Congress passed a law naming three federal employees thought to be disloyal to the United States. The law ordered that these employees receive no salary until the president reappointed them and the Senate reapproved their appointments. The court held that this law violated the Constitution.

Laws that punish people for acts that were not crimes at the time they were performed are called *ex post facto laws.* They are outlawed by the Constitution. Suppose you read a book from the library and the school board decided later that the book should not be available to students your age. If you were punished for reading the book, your punishment would be ex post facto.

A *writ of habeas corpus* is an order to explain to a judge why law enforcement officials are holding a person in custody. It prevents a person from being kept in jail without cause. It is a very important limit on the power of government because it forces the government either to charge a suspect with a crime or let the person go. Because of the writ of habeas corpus, the government cannot just lock up people with whom it disagrees.

As you read the Constitution, pay close attention to the language describing relationships among the states, national government, and the people. At times, the authors used language that was very specific. They did this to make sure everyone knew precisely what the rules meant. At other times, they wrote very general statements. They did this to give the Constitution flexibility to meet changing times and circumstances. This combination of detail and generality is one of the reasons why the Constitution has been able to last for so many years.

The United States has no nobility like the English royal family.

CHAPTER ACTIVITIES

Do You Know?

1. Which of the following is the best example of the constitutional requirement of full faith and credit among states? (a) returning escaped fugitives, (b) letting visitors to the state serve on juries, (c) helping to put down a riot in another state, (d) recognizing an out-of-state birth certificate as valid.

2. Which of the following are exclusive powers of the national government? (a) taxing exports, (b) declaring war, (c) regulating interstate commerce, (d) determining how elections shall be held.

3. Under the Constitution, the President of the United States has the power to (a) regulate the postal service, (b) make rules affecting naturalization, (c) veto laws, (d) raise taxes.

4. Which of the following powers does the Constitution give to Congress? (a) granting pardons, (b) borrowing money, (c) setting up patents to protect inventors, (d) making rules relating to bankuptcy.

5. Where do impeachment proceedings against a President of the United States originate? (a) in the Senate, (b) at the Supreme Court, (c) in the House of Representatives, (d) in state legislatures.

6. Which of the following activities are prohibited by the Constitution? (a) granting noble titles, (b) passing bills of attainder, (c) enacting ex post facto laws, (d) putting down a domestic insurrection.

For Discussion

1. What are the advantages and disadvantages of having the national government and the state share certain powers?

2. Do you think Congress was correct in admitting states that were not geographically part of the United States? Explain your answer.

3. Do you think the federal courts have the power to hear too many different types of cases? Give the reasons for your answer.

Research

1. Make a list of the things you eat. Try to determine which of them may have been involved in interstate commerce and which in intrastate commerce.

2. According to Article I, Section 8 of the Constitution, the Congress has the power to grant *letters of marque and reprisal.* Look in the Glossary and find out what the term means.

Playing Roles

Suppose some students are justices of the Supreme Court during the 1850's. Others are lawyers for a northern state and still others are lawyers for a southern state. The court must decide whether a slave who ran away to the northern state should be returned to the southern state.

★

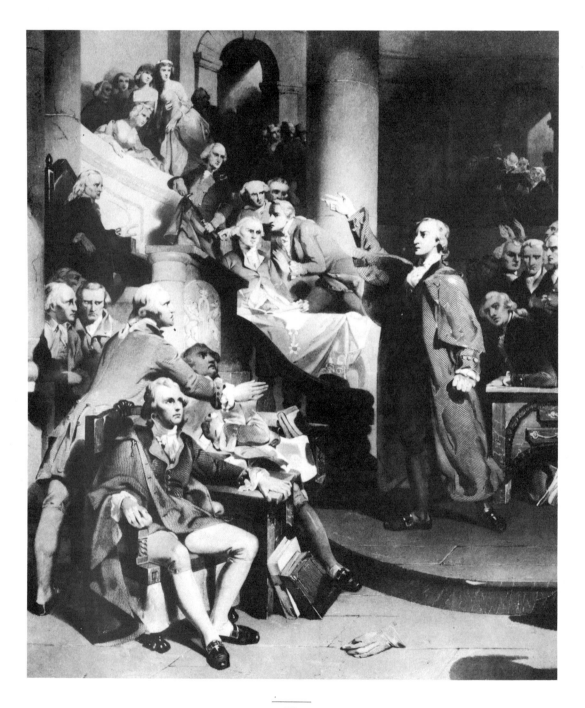

⑤

ADDING A BILL OF RIGHTS

Remember how delighted you were when you got your own bicycle? You could ride it all over the neighborhood much more quickly than you could walk. However, you needed to remember the safety rules. That way you didn't have an accident and hurt pedestrians or yourself. What might have happened if nobody bothered to tell you the rules? What if everyone took those rules so much for granted that no one even wrote them down? How could you watch out for pedestrians' rights if you weren't sure what those rights were?

When the delegates sought to have the new Constitution ratified, they faced a similar problem. They thought everyone knew what individual rights were, so they did not define them in the Constitution. However, the lack of specific guarantees of personal liberty was one of the main reasons why a number of states were reluctant to accept the Constitution.

Objections to the Constitution

In order to approve the new Constitution, voters were to elect representatives to special state conventions. In New York, Virginia, and Massachusetts, the people and their representatives were strongly opposed to the Constitution. They were called the *Antifederalists*. The Antifederalists included such patriots as Patrick Henry, the Virginia orator; Sam Adams, the Massachusetts agitator; George Mason, who had written much of the Virginia Constitution; and Richard Henry Lee, who had served as Virginia's delegate to the Continental Congress.

Antifederalist Patrick Henry was a fiery orator.

53

The Antifederalists argued that the states would be absorbed into an all-too-powerful national government. They claimed that the limits on direct voting and the long terms of the president and senators would create an aristocratic class. They also feared that the president might become another monarch. In other words, these Antifederalists felt that the new Constitution was most undemocratic.

Their major objection to the new Constitution was its lack of a bill of rights. *Bills of rights* list the specific freedoms that governments cannot threaten or take away. When the Constitution was being written, many state constitutions already had bills of rights. For that reason, the authors of the Constitution did not feel it was necessary to have another one. The Antifederalists believed that without a list of personal freedoms, the new national government might abuse its powers. They worried that it would destroy the liberties won in the Revolution.

Supporters of the Constitution

Supporters of the new system were called *Federalists.* They included George Washington and two future Supreme Court Chief Justices, John Marshall and John Jay. To help win support for the new Constitution, Alexander Hamilton, James Madison, and John Jay wrote a series of essays for the newspapers. These were eventually published under the title *The Federalist.*

In these essays they described the Constitution and explained how it would work. They answered its critics calmly and effectively. They pointed out how the new government was a republic with safeguards against monarchy. They told how federalism offered the states an important role in government. They told how representative democracy gave the citizens a voice in their government. Finally, they explained how checks and balances and

Two Federalists: John Marshall, who came to be known as "The Great Chief Justice" (above), and John Jay (left).

separation of powers were safeguards against the abuse of power.

By the end of July 1788, 11 states had ratified the Constitution. The new government could go into effect. North Carolina and Rhode Island did not approve the Constitution until after the government was set up. However, the Antifederalists' criticisms were not ignored. As soon as the new Congress met, the legislature, under the leadership of Madison, prepared 10 *amendments,* or additions, to the Constitution. They were all approved by 1791 and became known as the Bill of Rights.

The First Amendment

The First Amendment is perhaps the most important part of the Bill of Rights. It protects five of the most basic liberties. They are freedom of religion, freedom of speech, freedom of the press, freedom of assembly, and freedom to petition the government to right wrongs. These were the guarantees that the Antifederalists missed most in the new Constitution.

Freedom of religion. Freedom of religion means that the government may not force you to accept one set of religious beliefs nor may it interfere with the way you worship.

One of the most heated debates of our time involves the issue of prayer and schools. Do students have the right to pray in class? Or would a prayer interfere with another student's right *not* to pray? A number of cases have been brought before the Supreme Court to settle this matter. The Supreme Court has held that prayers or even a moment of silence would violate the principles of the First Amendment.

Freedom of speech. This freedom entitles American citizens to say what they think, provided they do not intentionally hurt someone else's reputation by making false accusations. Neither may they make irresponsible statements deliberately harmful to others, such as yelling, "Fire!" in a crowded theater when there is no fire. There are many issues about which Americans disagree, from child-rearing practices to baseball teams to Presidential candidates. Freedom of speech enables people to state their opinions openly to try to convince others to change their minds.

The First Amendment also gives you the right to disagree with what others say without fear of punishment by government authorities. However, if you make an outrageous statement, such as, "The earth is flat," free speech will not keep people from making fun of you. If you express an unpopular opinion — for exam-

An Amish girl walks home from school. The First Amendment protects all religious traditions.

ple, that students do not get enough homework — don't be surprised if your classmates avoid you. The First Amendment does not prevent social or peer pressure to conform to what others think.

Freedom of the press. This freedom makes it possible for Americans to keep informed about what is going on in government. It helps them to be responsible citizens. Reporters and editors can criticize the government without risk of punishment, provided they do not deliberately tell lies. Newspapers, magazines, and books, as well as television and movie scripts, do not have to be submitted for government inspection before they are published. This censorship would violate the First Amendment.

Antiwar demonstrations exercise their rights of free speech and assembly during a 1971 march.

Freedom of assembly. This freedom makes it possible for Americans to join clubs or political parties, even if those groups represent unpopular views. Because of the First Amendment, people can join groups to promote animal rights, the nuclear freeze, or conservation. They can join groups to protest apartheid in South Africa, imported clothing and shoes, toxic wastes, or aid to Nicaraguan or Salvadoran rebels. By sharing common interests, Americans can learn to work together. There are groups devoted to the interests of young people. Scout troops and 4-H clubs are but two examples.

Freedom to petition. This important freedom allows people to tell the government what they think is needed. They can try to get the government to do what they want. Or they can try to prevent the government from acting in a certain way. They can complain to the government without fear of penalty when things aren't going the way they should. For example, if people dump garbage near your school, you and your parents can petition the government to clean it up. Freedom to petition helps the government as well. It lets government know how well it is doing its job.

The Right to Bear Arms

The Second Amendment guarantees that citizens may "keep and bear arms." In other words, your family may own a gun, subject to state licensing laws. The gun can be used for protection, such as frightening away burglars. It can also be used for recreational activities, such as hunting. Because criminals often use unlicensed weapons to hurt others, some people have urged the national government to control the sale of guns. Other people have argued that gun control is a violation of the Second Amendment.

Housing Troops

The Third Amendment pledges that in peacetime, citizens will never have to keep soldiers in their homes without consenting. Before the Revolution, the British forced Americans to provide lodging and food for their troops. The colonists bitterly resented this intrusion on their privacy as well as the cost of feeding hungry soldiers.

Searches and Seizures

The Fourth through Eighth Amendments concern the rights of people suspected of crime. The Fourth Amendment protects citizens from improper searches of their bodies, possessions, or homes. It requires that a detailed warrant be issued by a judge listing what can be searched. There has to be a good reason for the search. For example, suppose the police knew that someone in your school was selling drugs. The Constitution does not let them search the home of every student. In fact, they could not search the homes of even one or two students without a court order.

Rights of the Accused

The Fifth Amendment protects the rights of anyone accused of a crime. It assumes that everyone is innocent until proven guilty. In some countries, exactly the opposite is true. Suspects must prove that they are innocent. When a person is accused of a crime for which the punishment could be death, the Fifth Amendment requires that a *grand jury* look at the charges before that person can be brought trial. A grand jury is a group of citizens who decide if there is enough evidence to try a person. It is intended to prevent people from being falsely accused of a serious crime. Today, grand juries consider most serious criminal charges. The Fifth Amendment also states that the person cannot be tried twice for the same crime.

The section of the Fifth Amendment that has received the most publicity is the guarantee against *self-incrimination.* This means people cannot be forced to testify against themselves. Under the Fifth Amendment, law enforcement officials must produce the evidence necessary to convict a person of a crime. The accused person cannot be made to provide it. In earlier times, people were tortured until they confessed to crimes they may not even have committed. The guarantee against self-incrimination makes sure that unfair pressure cannot be used to make a person confess.

In the 1950's, this section of the Fifth Amendment sparked a public uproar. Notorious criminals accused of having ties with the underworld claimed the Fifth Amendment protected them from having to testify. If they had denied those accusations, they probably would have been found guilty of *perjury,* or lying under oath. Perjury is punishable by law. If they had told the truth, they would have risked punishment. Instead, they refused to testify on the grounds that they might incriminate themselves. Law enforcement officials had to come up with evidence against them or free them.

Racketeer Frank Costello (right), was fined in 1954 for abusing the Fifth Amendment to avoid giving testimony.

The right to remain silent also protects innocent people. During the 1950's, the government became concerned about Communists. Politicians held hearings in which people were asked which organizations they had joined and who their friends were. If they answered that they had been involved in certain groups or friendships, they were accused of being Communists. At times, the accusations became wild and unfounded. Many people took refuge in the Fifth Amendment protection against self-incrimination. Some, perhaps, were Communists who might have wished to see the government overthrown. Others, however, were innocent citizens who had been caught up in a hysterical movement. The Constitution protected them against ruthless accusations.

Due Process of Law

Another section of the Fifth Amendment holds that "no one can be deprived of life, liberty, or property without due process of law." In other words, the government must follow certain legal procedures before deciding on a penalty. It can't jail person because it suspects that the person committed a crime. It must prove the accusation by following certain rules and methods. However, "due process of law" is a rather vague and general term. As times have changed, so has its meaning.

In the 1930's, photographers and newsreel cameramen were allowed to record trials. (There was no television news.) The trial of a man accused of kidnapping the aviator Charles Lindbergh's child, took on the atmosphere of a circus. Lawyers and witnesses

Charles Lindbergh testifies during the unruly trial of the man accused of kidnapping his child.

became more interested in creating publicity than in determining justice. They began to make exaggerated claims.

In later years, to discourage publicity stunts and other distractions, only artists and reporters were allowed to be present in court. Now some judges permit television cameras to record trials. How might the presence or absence of cameras affect a defendant's right to due process?

Eminent Domain

Finally, the Fifth Amendment requires the government to pay citizens when it takes over their property for a public use. The government's right to take this property is called *eminent domain.* Suppose the state wanted to build a highway which would run right through your residence. It would have to pay the owners a reasonable price for the property. The government could force you to move, but at least it would have to provide you with the money to relocate.

Fair and Speedy Trials

The Sixth Amendment provides more requirements for a fair trial in criminal cases. It guarantees a speedy, public trial by an impartial jury in the area where the crime was committed. The defendant must be able to question the accusers and to force favorable witnesses to testify. The accused has a right to a lawyer.

How would you feel if you were falsely accused of cheating on a test? Suppose you had no idea who was accusing you. How could you question your accuser? How could you defend yourself? Your reputation could be hurt if you had to wait a long time before the matter was cleared up. Wouldn't you want a chance to prove your innocence? This is why the Sixth Amendment is so important.

Jury Trials

The Seventh Amendment guarantees that Americans will receive a jury trial in civil (as opposed to criminal) cases involving property worth more than $20. Today, however, people do not bring such cases to federal courts unless a much larger sum of money is involved.

Bails, Fines, and Punishment

The Eighth Amendment protects people from having to pay unreasonably high *bail* in order to be released from prison before they go to trial. Bail is money given to pledge that a person accused of a crime will appear for trial. The Eighth Amendment also protects people from unreasonably high fines. Finally, it outlaws cruel and unusual punishment. This requirement, as well as the Fifth Amendment's guarantee against self-incrimination, protects citizens from the use of torture. Some people have argued that the death penalty is a form of cruel and unusual punishment.

Reserved Powers

The last two amendments address the liberties of citizens and the rights of states. The Ninth Amendment states that the Constitution and the Bill of Rights do not define all of the fundamental rights people have. Such rights exist whether or not they are defined. The Tenth Amendment makes a similar claim concerning the rights of the states. It holds that the states and the people have powers that are set aside and not listed item by item. These powers are called *reserved powers*. They can be contrasted with *express powers,* which are specifically defined in the Constitution.

In this way the Constitution allows for growth and change. With the invention of radio, movies, television, automobiles, jet planes, computers, and satellites, what rights might the states and the people now claim? How else can the Constitution be kept up to date?

These defense workers in 1941 were demonstrating their patriotism.

CHAPTER ACTIVITIES

Do You Know?

Match the rights and amendment numbers.

The right to keep and bear arms

The rights to a grand jury trial, due process of law, protection from self-incrimination, and payment for eminent domain

Freedom of religion, speech, the press, assembly

The right to petition, the right to a speedy, public, fair trial

Protection from forced housing of troops in private homes

Grants reserved powers to the states

Protection from unreasonable bail and fines and from cruel and unusual punishment

Gives people rights not defined in the Constitution

The right to a jury trial in civil cases involving property worth more than $20

Protection from improper searches and seizures

1

2

3

4

5

6

7

8

9

10

For Discussion

1. If you were drawing up a bill of rights today, which rights would you include and which would you omit? Give reasons for your answer.

2. Why do many people consider the First Amendment to be the most important part of the Bill of Rights?

3. What parts of the Bill of Rights apply to radio, television, movies, and computers? Explain your answer.

Research

Read sections of *The Federalist* and list some of the arguments you find.

Role Playing

Divide the class into two teams: The Federalists and the Antifederalists. Present arguments for and against the adoption of the Constitution.

*These 1,000 new citizens
in San Francisco were sworn in
via satellite on July 4, 1986.*

6

KEEPING THE CONSTITUTION UP TO DATE:
FORMAL AMENDMENTS

I t is very cold outside, so you go put on your winter coat. Much to your surprise, it no longer fits. The sleeves are too short. You've grown since the last time you wore the coat. What can you do? One solution is to buy a new coat. However, you might prefer your old coat. It is comfortable, you like the color, and you know that it keeps you warm. You might get someone to alter the coat by letting down the sleeves. This would be easier and far less expensive than having to buy a new coat.

The people of the United States have taken a similar approach to their Constitution. The country has certainly grown since 1787. Just think of how much more land the United States occupies today. There are now 50 states, with two that are not even part of the mainland. There are also territories, such as Puerto Rico, with ties to the United States.

Many more people live in the United States today than in 1787. In 1790, for example, the population totaled slightly less than 4 million. Today it is approximately 240 million. The nation has al-

ways welcomed people who come here from other lands, such as Britain, the Scandinavian countries, Holland, France, and Spain. Some come from independent nations that did not even exist in 1787, such as Zimbabwe, Guyana, and the Philippines. Today's Americans represent many more countries and cultures than they did in 1787. They have more ideas about what is the best way for families to get along, what foods taste best, what jobs they want, and what government should do.

Production of goods and services is another measurement of growth. Since 1790, the value of goods and services produced in the United States has increased over 120 times! (This is called the *Gross National Product.*) Just think of how much Americans have achieved in terms of energy, products, and skills. For example, gasoline-powered automobiles and trucks have replaced horse-drawn carriages and wagons. Dirt roads, harness-makers, and blacksmiths have almost disappeared. People have become used to traffic lights, paved highways, shopping malls, fast-food restaurants, video games, and suburban living.

While the United States has grown, its people have kept their Constitution. It is comfortable, they like it, and they know it works. Rather than write a new constitution every time the nation grows, they make alterations. They prefer the known to a new, untried system of government. The Constitution has even survived a Civil War in the 1860's when the northern states fought to prevent the southern states from leaving the union.

The Amending Process

What has enabled the Constitution to adapt to all these circumstances? Much like a coat, it can be altered when the country grows and changes. The Constitution itself describes one process by which it can be modified — by amendment. Two-thirds of Congress can propose changes. Or two-thirds of the state legislatures can ask Congress to call a convention to propose changes. This second method has never been used. Three-fourths of the state legislatures or specially assembled state conventions would have to ratify the changes. Ratifying state conventions were used only once, two pass the 21st Amendment.

Extending Voting Rights

Many amendments have helped to keep the Constitution up-to-date. They reveal how much attitudes have changed since the country was founded. Amendments have made it possible for more Americans to vote for their government. As times changed, people no longer accepted the idea that only white men over the age of 21 were qualified to elect officials. They also decided that the Senate should be elected directly by the voters. They resented unreasonable obstacles some of the states set up to prevent people from voting. They wanted the United States to truly become a representative democracy.

Voters at racially-mixed polls in 1959. In this special election, majorities voted for the removal of three segregationist school board members.

The Constitution has been expanded to allow blacks, women, and 18-year-olds to vote.

As a result, the Constitution was amended several times to give more people the right to vote. The 15th Amendment (1870) was passed to permit blacks to vote — although it took almost a century before the amendment's promise was kept. (The 13th Amendment [1865] freed slaves after the Civil War, and the 14th Amendment [1868] made them citizens.) The 19th Amendment (1920) let women vote. The 23rd Amendment (1961) allowed residents of the District of Columbia to help elect the president and vice-president. The 26th Amendment (1971) finally gave 18-, 19-, and 20-year-olds a chance to vote. Eighteen-year-olds have always been considered old enough to fight for their country, and it seemed unfair to deny them a say in who the nation's leaders would be.

Other amendments widened voters' choices and removed unreasonable obstacles to voting. The 17th Amendment (1913) gave citizens, rather than state legislators, the right to elect senators. The 24th Amendment (1964) did away with poll taxes and other fees charged at the voting booth. These measures had been used to keep blacks from voting.

As the nation grew, more and more Americans gained a voice in government. They were given the right to make decisions about matters important to them. You choose your own friends, select your own clothes, pick some of the subjects you study, and develop your own interests and hobbies. As you grow older, you gain the right to make more decisions about the things that are important to you. Eventually, you, too, will vote. Amendments have guaranteed your right to do so.

Other Changes

Other amendments have affected the relationship between the national government and its citizens. For example, the 11th Amendment (1795) said that state courts, rather than federal courts, should try suits involving parties of different states. The Constitution originally sent them to federal court. Cases arising between a state and a citizen of a different state, or between a state and a citizen of a foreign country, are also tried in state courts. As the nation grew and lawsuits increased, the 11th Amendment was needed to lighten the load of the federal courts.

Income Tax. Under the 16th Amendment (1913), the national government can charge citizens an income tax. Citizens must contribute some of the money they earn to help the government meet its expenses. The government uses taxpayers' money to help the country grow and expand. Programs, for example, in health, farming, labor, transportation, and education, have benefited many Americans. Income taxes have also paid for some of the costs of wars and the development of a modern system of defense.

Have you ever tried to stretch your allowance to cover the costs of afterschool snacks, movies, and gifts? What do you do when the money you receive isn't enough? Do you ask your parents for more? Do you try to earn money on your own? Imagine the difficulties the national government would have faced in meeting its expenses without an income tax.

Government agents disposing of illegal liquor during Prohibition.

Prohibition. The 18th Amendment (1919) gave the government power to prevent Americans from making, purchasing, or transporting alcoholic beverages. This is known as Prohibition. The national government had many troubles in trying to get people to stop drinking. The cocktail hour had become an important part of American life. Bars, nightclubs, and restaurants were accustomed to serving drinks.

Getting people to change their habits can be difficult. People who bite their nails, crack their knuckles, or chew the ends of their pencils can tell you how hard it is to stop. If they are scolded, many will continue the habit, but possibly only in private.

The 18th Amendment was very difficult to enforce. People did not stop drinking alcoholic beverages. Instead, they got them illegally. Crimes involving the sale and manufacture of alcohol increased. For example, people died from poisoned whiskey. When it became clear that the nation was unable to enforce the 18th Amendment, the Constitution was changed again. The 21st Amendment (1933) *repealed,* or cancelled, Prohibition.

Changing Election Methods

Some amendments have changed the terms and responsibilities of the president and vice president. The 12th Amendment (1804) alters presidential and vice presidential elections. It was needed because the authors of the Constitution did not foresee the rise of political parties. *Political parties* are groups of people who select candidates to run for office to promote their interests. Originally, the candidate who got the most votes in the electoral college became president, and the runner-up became vice president. Once political parties came into being, this made it possible for a president to represent one party and a vice president another. If there were a tie in the electoral college, the House of Representatives was to choose the president.

What would happen if the candidates with the most popular votes were of one political party and the House was controlled by another party? Would the wishes of the voters and the electors be carried out? This problem arose when Republican Thomas Jefferson ran for president in 1800 with Aaron Burr as his running mate. Jefferson and Burr received the same number of electoral votes. The Federalist-controlled House almost chose Burr to embarrass Jefferson. To prevent this from happening again, the 12th Amendment required that separate electoral votes be cast for the president and the vice president.

Lame Duck Amendment. The 20th Amendment (1933) shortened the time between the election and inauguration of a president. It also changed the timing of congressional sessions. Originally, the president and Congress were elected in November, but they did not take office until March. There was always the risk that those who had lost the elections would pass unpopular laws during the four months they remained in office. More commonly, they did very little during that time because they had been voted out of office. They no longer represented the will of the people. As a result, they were called lame ducks. Their wings had been clipped by the voters. The 20th Amendment is known as the Lame Duck Amendment.

Limited terms. The 22nd Amendment (1951) limited presidents to two full terms of office. President Washington started the tradition of serving only two terms. But in the 1930's and 1940's, people voted Franklin Roosevelt into office four times. Some Americans objected to that break with tradition. They helped to pass an amendment to limit presidents to two terms.

You have probably experienced a similar limit yourself, if you had a teacher you especially liked in one grade and wanted the same teacher in the next grade. Occasionally, teachers continue with their students. But for the most part, at the beginning of the school year, a class is assigned to a different teacher. This is done so that you can experience a variety of teaching styles. You will learn more from some than from others. What is good for you may not be good for all of your classmates. If you had the same teacher all the time, you would become accustomed to each other. Things would get comfortably predictable, but would you learn as much?

Illness and Vacancies. The 25th Amendment (1967) explains what to do if the vice presidency becomes vacant or if the president becomes ill. Neither problem was addressed in the Constitution. From time to time, presidents became ill while in office. For example, Woodrow Wilson had a stroke. No provision was made for a chief executive in the event that he lived but did not recover. When a vacancy in the vice presidency occurred in the 1970's, the 25th Amendment was used for the first time. Vice President Spiro Agnew had to leave office. Then President Nixon nominated Gerald Ford for vice president, and a majority in Congress accepted his choice. The amendment was used again when Nixon resigned, and Ford became president. Nelson Rockefeller was chosen as Ford's vice president.

In 1985 Ronald Reagan became a "lame duck" president.

In 1985, when President Ronald Reagan had surgery for cancer, the 25th Amendment was used for a third time. It explains what to do when a president is temporarily too sick to work. The vice president becomes the acting president in order to carry on the business of the country. So, for a short time, Vice President George Bush was acting president.

Will there be other amendments to the Constitution? Probably, as times change and people have different needs. In 1972, the Equal Rights Amendment was proposed so that men and women would be treated equally. However, it was not ratified by three-fourths of the states.

The amending process takes so long and is so complicated that it has only been used 26 times in 200 years. Perhaps the founders did not want people to make too many changes in the system they created. So they discouraged them by making it difficult to amend the Constitution. However, Americans have found other ways to keep their government up-to-date.

CHAPTER ACTIVITIES

Do You Know?

1. Match the voters and the amendments that affected them:

Residents of the District of Columbia	15
Black Americans	19
18-, 19-, and 20-year-olds	26
Women	23

2. What did the 17th Amendment do? (a) end poll taxes, (b) allow the direct election of senators, (c) set up an income tax, (d) ban the sale of alcoholic beverages.

3. Which of the following amendments are concerned with the presidency? (a) the 12th, (b) the 22nd, (c) the 11th, (d) the 25th.

4. What did the 20th Amendment do? (a) repeal an earlier amendment, (b) change electoral college methods, (c) limit a president to two terms, (d) change the date officials take office after election.

For Discussion

1. Do you think the procedure for adding amendments to the Constitution is a good one? Give reasons for your answer.

2. In what other ways might the Constitution be amended? Do you think such amendments would be ratified?

Research

1. Read the 13th, 14th, and 15th Amendments.

2. Woodrow Wilson, Dwight Eisenhower, and Lyndon Johnson became ill during their presidencies. Find out what was done to run the government while they were disabled.

Role Playing

Suppose you are members of Congress. You have to decide whether to propose an amendment to allow prayers in school. Some of you argue in favor of the amendment while others take the opposite side.

$$\text{(7)}$$

KEEPING THE CONSTITUTION UP TO DATE:

INFORMAL METHODS

Suppose you want your parents to change the way they treat you. They may not recognize that you are growing up. If you demand more privileges you probably will not convince them that you have indeed changed. However, you may be more successful if you use informal methods. Instead of demanding your rights, you can show them indirectly how much you've grown up.

Little by little, you can get your parents to treat you differently. One way you can do this is to take on more responsibilities. You might do some household chores without being asked. You might do your homework without waiting for them to remind you.

Similarly, the Constitution has been altered informally as new rules and organizations developed to get things done. Customs, presidential actions, laws, and court judgments have brought about this gradual change in the government. As a result, much has been added to the Constitution without formal amendments.

Customs

One way that the Constitution has been brought up to date is by custom. Customs are routine ways of doing things that people come to accept as natural. You and your family share certain customs concerning the celebration of special holidays. You may send cards or gifts. You may eat a special cake. Nowhere is it written down that you and your family must do this. Probably no one in your family deliberately decided what to do. Instead, your celebrations have developed over time into a set of joyous customs.

By custom, certain routines have gradually been added to the government created by the Constitution. For example, political parties are an important part of American elections. The founders did not expect political parties to develop. Shortly after the Constitution was ratified, parties grew up around ideas about the kind of society the United States should become.

One group wanted the United States to remain a nation of farmers. Thomas Jefferson, James Madison, and their supporters formed the Democrat-Republican party to support rural interests. Another group wanted the country to develop into a nation of manufacturers. Alexander Hamilton, John Adams, and their supporters founded the Federalist party to advance commercial interests.

The leaders of each group met to select candidates for office to support their views. This method of choosing candidates was known as a *caucus.* Later, *nominating conventions* made up of many delegates met to choose candidates. Then *primaries* were held so that loyal party voters could help pick candidates. But you will find no mention of parties, caucuses, conventions, or primaries in the Constitution.

Nominating conventions, such as the 1980 Democratic Convention, are not mentioned in the Constitution.

President Carter meets with Secretary of Energy Charles Duncan.

Presidents' Actions

Presidents have also added organizations and routines to the government. For example, although the Constitution gave Congress the power to create heads of executive departments, it did not describe the president's *cabinet.* President Washington set up the first cabinet. It included the heads of executive departments, called *secretaries,* who met to discuss programs and to manage the business of government. In Washington's cabinet were the secretaries of state, war, the treasury, and the attorney general.

Membership in the cabinet keeps changing. Since Washington's time, many departments have been added. For example, we now have a secretary of housing and urban affairs, a secretary of health and human services, and a secretary of transportation. A secretary of energy first joined the cabinet under President Jimmy Carter in the 1970's. The cabinet has grown with the country.

In addition, other executive organizations have developed to help carry out presidential responsibilities. The White House Staff and the Executive Office of the President help supervise the executive branch. They guide and coordinate the cabinet departments and other groups so that the laws are "faithfully executed," or put into effect. In Washington's day, these organizations did not exist.

Presidents have gradually changed the way the government set up by the Constitution works. Since President Wilson's term of office (1912–1920), presidents have traveled abroad to visit other heads of state. While the presidents are out of the country, they are still in charge of the nation. The vice president does not take over. The Constitution says nothing about who runs the government when a president leaves the United States. (Modern communications and air travel make this easier than when presidents traveled by ship and received most of the messages by cable.)

Another important development has been the growth of presidential power. Presidents Andrew Jackson, Abraham Lincoln, Theodore Roosevelt, and Franklin Roosevelt were very active leaders. They set an example for other presidents to follow. During national crises, they took charge and fully exerted the powers of the presidency. Under Jackson's leadership, more Americans were able to vote and run for office. Lincoln's presidency sought to keep the Union from dissolving in civil war. Under Theodore Roosevelt, many needed reforms were passed, and the nation became respected as a world power. His cousin Franklin Roosevelt faced the challenges of a nationwide economic collapse and a world war. In a nuclear age, when decisions about war and peace may have to be made very quickly, strong, active presidents have become even more important.

The vice presidency was created primarily to replace a president who dies in office. The Constitution says the vice president presides over the Senate and votes in case of a tie. Otherwise, it says little about the vice president's duties.

For a long time, vice presidents did very little. Most people didn't even know their names. In modern times, though, presidents have encouraged vice presidents to be more active. They have represented the nation on diplomatic missions and at important events. Sometimes they sit in on cabinet meetings. As vice president, Lyndon Johnson played an important role in supervising the space program.

Congressional Changes

Congress has helped to keep the Constitution up-to-date. The founders provided for this. First of all, they required Congress to set up the court system. As you have already learned, Congress created district courts to try cases, and circuit courts to hear appeals. It set up a number of other specialized courts as well.

Secondly, the Constitution encourages the Congress to expand its powers. The Constitution's *elastic clause* stretches definitions of what Congress may do. It gives Congress authority to make all laws "necessary and proper" to carry out its duties. These are called *implied powers.* These powers make it possible for Congress to adapt to changing times.

When your parents tell you to do what you think is best to carry out their wishes, you are being encouraged to stretch instructions. You are being given the right to determine what is appropriate to the situation. In a sense, you are defining your own powers and interpreting the way they should be applied.

Under the elastic clause, Congress created a number of *independent agencies,* such as the Federal Communications Commission (FCC). In defining what these organizations were to do, Congress did not follow the principle of separation of powers. The agencies use executive powers when they carry out congressional laws. For example, the FCC may order broadcasters to give candidates for president equal time to present their views to the public. However, agencies also make legislative decisions. Usually, Congress asks the agencies to fill in all the details of the laws it passes. The FCC "makes laws" when it decides that certain words may not be used in programs. Finally, the agencies serve as courts. For example, the FCC holds hearings to determine whether or not to renew the license of a television station.

Historically, Congress has used the elastic clause to broaden its powers. It has used it to regulate commerce and to tax and spend for the public welfare. In this way it has been able to meet the needs of a growing industrial nation and its people. Other congressional powers have been stretched as well.

Since Congress can regulate the currency, it claimed the power to create a national bank. The bank issued paper money, held monies collected by taxes, and paid the government's expenses. It also lent money to private banks. In the case of *McCulloch* v. *Maryland* (1819), Congress's right to set up this bank was upheld by the Supreme Court. (Today the functions once performed by the national bank are carried out by other government organizations.)

President Johnson salutes the Apollo 8 astronauts.

Court Interpretations

McCulloch v. *Maryland* shows another important way the Constitution has changed — through judicial decisions. Court decisions reflect the changing needs of the country. Throughout much of American history, the courts have been asked to rule whether acts of Congress, the president, or the states conflict with the Constitution. When the courts decide whether or not such acts are constitutional, they are exercising *judicial review.*

The Constitution itself is silent on the matter of how it is to be interpreted. Nowhere does it say that the Supreme Court may decide what is constitutional and what is not. The Court took on that power in 1803 in the case of *Marbury* v. *Madison.* Chief Justice John Marshall ruled that part of an act of Congress was unconstitutional.

He reasoned that since the Constitution is the supreme law of the land, judges should interpret that law. Since then, if laws passed by Congress seem to conflict with the Constitution, the courts decide which law stands. The Supreme Court makes the final judgment on constitutional questions. Those who disagree with its opinions may try to amend the Constitution to reverse the Court's decision.

In ruling whether or not a law is constitutional, the courts must interpret the wording of the Constitution. They are able to do this because the language in many sections of the Constitution is unclear or very general. For example, what do the words "necessary and proper" actually mean?

Strict constructionists of the Constitution define the terms very narrowly. They want the power of government limited by the actual words in the Constitution. They are less likely to be concerned with changing circumstances. *Loose constructionists* are more likely to define those terms very broadly. They believe that

A segregated waiting room at a Memphis bus station in 1943.

the national government should be strong and powerful. They are more likely to favor adjustments to new conditions. Over time, Supreme Court rulings have gradually stretched the meaning of the Constitution to cover new circumstances. Supreme Court decisions made it possible for government to regulate business as the nation became industrial. New technology has required new interpretations of the Bill of Rights. The authors of the Constitution never imagined radio, movies, and television. The courts extended freedom of the press to include them. Other difficult questions arise. For example, are satellite broadcasts and citizens' band radio transmissions covered by freedom of the press?

Changing Interpretation

Two famous Supreme Court decisions about civil rights show how the Constitution's meaning has been adapted over time. They are *Plessy* v. *Ferguson* (1896) and *Brown* v. *The Board of Education of Topeka* (1954).

Plessy was a black man who sued to have the right to sit in a railroad car reserved for white people. In those days, in the South, the black and white races were segregated, or kept apart. State and local laws prevented members of the two races from using the same restrooms, drinking fountains, restaurants and schools. The Supreme Court ruled — against Plessy — that segregation was constitutional as long as each race was given equal facilities. In fact, facilities for blacks were almost always worse than those for whites. Nevertheless, the principle of "separate but equal" was the law.

In 1954, another black man, Oliver Brown, sued to have his daughter Linda attend a nearby white elementary school. She was traveling a mile each day to attend a black elementary school. The Supreme Court ruled unanimously (every justice agreed) that segregated schools were unequal. Even if the schools were equal in

A young black girl being escorted to a recently desegregated school.

size, space and equipment, segregation deprived black children of an equal opportunity to learn. The justices said segregation would encourage them to feel inferior to white children.

Between 1896 and 1954, attitudes had changed. People were realizing how unjust keeping the races apart was. The Supreme Court interpreted the Constitution to adjust to this change. Since 1954, a number of laws and court decisions have made the Constitution truly "color-blind."

For the past 200 years, the Constitution has grown and changed with the United States and its people. Some critics argue that the Constitution is so flexible that it has lost its meaning. Others insist that the Constitution is worth preserving.

CHAPTER ACTIVITIES

Do You Know?

1. Which of the following are informal ways the Constitution can be kept up to date? (a) developing customs, (b) passing amendments, (c) interpreting laws, (d) using implied powers.

2. Which of the following are not mentioned in the Constitution? (a) the president's cabinet, (b) political parties, (c) independent agencies, (d) the Supreme Court.

3. The Constitution says nothing about (a) heads of departments, (b) the Executive Office of the President, (c) presidential trips abroad, (d) the White House Staff.

4. Which of the following has enabled Congress to expand its own legislative powers? (a) strict constructionists, (b) the elastic clause, (c) primaries, (d) nominating conventions.

5. Which of the following best describes judicial review? (a) making laws that arc necessary and proper to govern the nation, (b) seeing that the laws are faithfully executed, (c) deciding whether laws violate the Constitution, (d) recommending laws to Congress.

For Discussion

1. Do you think that the executive branch of government has become too powerful? Give reasons for your answer.

2. Explain why you think political parties are so important to Americans.

3. Do you think that Congress has abused its implied powers? Why or why not?

Research

1. Look in an almanac and make a list of the independent agencies of the federal government.

2. Read the Supreme Court opinions in the cases of *Plessy* v. *Ferguson* and *Brown* v. *The Board of Education.* Share sections of these opinions with your class.

Role Playing

Divide the class into teams of strict constructionists and loose constructionists. Then debate whether the Constitution gave President Jefferson the power to purchase the Louisiana Territory.

★

8

LOOKING AHEAD

When you look at your family album, you see yourself as an infant, a toddler, a child, a preteen, and perhaps a teenager. You see the same face, the same eyes, the same hair. You wear different clothing, pose with different friends, grow taller or leaner. In some pictures you see yourself doing things you could not do in earlier snapshots, such as sitting, crawling, walking, jumping, climbing, or dancing. With all these changes, the photographs show the same familiar you.

Although it may offer some clues, your family album does not show how you will look in five or ten years. You can see your past much more easily than you can predict the future. So much that lies ahead is unknown. The career you may choose, who you may marry, how many children you may have, and where you will live, cannot be predicted by looking at old photographs.

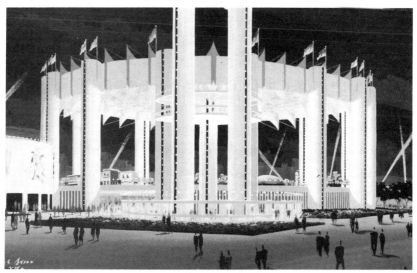

New York State's futuristic exhibit for a World's Fair.

For the same reasons, it is easier to see where the Constitution has been than to predict where it is going. The Constitution has survived a number of crises and changes, such as a civil war and economic depressions. Most probably, it will last for another 200 years.

There have been a number of proposals to alter the Constitution. These proposals are designed to make the national government more representative of a majority of the people.

Students of the Constitution constantly debate these proposals. Some believe that the Constitution should be changed because it holds back Americans. Others insist that preserving the Constitution as it is helps the Americans move forward. As you read the arguments on both sides, try to make up your own mind.

Changing Presidential Elections

The first proposal to modify the Constitution concerns the way the president is chosen. Since the president is elected by members of the electoral college, one popular idea for reform is to have direct presidential elections. In that way, the president would more truly be the peoples' choice. After all, the Senate was originally elected by state legislatures. Isn't it time to bring the election of the president up to date? In 1977, President Jimmy Carter supported this idea. However, the change was not made.

Supporters of the direct presidential election argue that the electoral college system does not accurately represent votes cast by the people. This is called the *popular vote*. Voters in states with the most electoral votes — such as New York, California, Illinois — have more influence than voters in states with few electoral votes, such as Montana and North Dakota.

There have been elections in which the will of the majority was misrepresented by the electoral college. In the election of 1888,

Benjamin Harrison had more electoral votes than Grover Cleveland. Harrison became president even though Cleveland had more popular votes. Moreover, under the present system, the House of Representatives decides who will be president when the electors can't. In 1800, when the electoral college was tied, the House chose Thomas Jefferson. In 1824, when no candidate received a majority, they chose John Quincy Adams.

There are arguments in favor of keeping the electoral college. Direct elections would give states with the largest populations an even greater voice than they now have. Presidential candidates would be more likely to ignore the needs of smaller, usually rural, states. The new system might distort the wishes of the majority even more. However, once the election was held, the results would be final.

ELECTORAL VOTES OF THE 50 STATES

Changing Terms

A second proposed change tries to make the government represent the wishes of the majority. It would require voters to elect all national officers at one time for four- or six-year terms. It is argued that this would let the government know what the majority wanted.

The plan would bridge the gap created by separation of powers. The founders arranged for the president and Congress to be elected at different times by different groups of voters. They did this to keep the executive and the legislative branches from acting together to deny citizens their freedoms.

Some argue that the founders were even more successful than they intended. Since the president and Congress often disagree, time may be wasted and opportunities lost. For example, in 1919, President Wilson proposed that the United States join the League of Nations. This international organization was designed to keep the peace at the end of World War I. The Senate rejected this proposal even though public opinion favored membership in this kind of organization. People have wondered whether the world would have been safer if the Senate had honored the people's wishes.

President Woodrow Wilson addressing Congress in April 1917.

How do you feel when you have to wait a long time for things to happen? When you are looking forward to getting back a test paper, quite often you grow impatient. Similarly, citizens may feel that the government takes too long to make decisions. If the president and Congress were elected at the same time for the same terms they might be more likely to cooperate and act faster.

On the other hand, uneven terms mean more elections. In that way, government gets fresh ideas about what people want. Since the whole government does not change with each election, experienced leaders can guide new ones. As a result, change is gradual rather than abrupt. If people are strongly divided on an issue, gradual change may be good. It allows time to adjust to new ways of doing things.

Compulsory Voting

A third proposal to change the Constitution concerns the right to vote. Today, all citizens over age 18 may vote. However, the Constitution does not force them to use that right. People who are uneducated, poor, or homeless often do not vote. Should all Americans of voting age be required to cast a ballot in national elections?

A major argument in favor of this proposal is that it would make the government truly represent the people. When you take part in an activity, you are more likely to care about the way it turns out. All the interests of Americans would be heard.

People often fail to vote because they feel they make little difference. They may be lazy or uncaring, or feel that they may be too ignorant to express their opinions. They may find it hard to prove citizenship or age. They may not even be able to go to the polling place. Even if they can get there, they may not know how to use a voting machine.

On the other hand, forcing Americans to vote won't necessarily overcome laziness or ignorance. It might be better to teach people how important their vote is and how to use it. People who don't care about voting are unlikely to vote wisely or carefully. Besides, freedom to vote also includes the freedom not to vote. In the United States, freedom means the right not to participate as well as the right to participate.

Are there times that you would prefer to watch your friends play after school rather than join them? Perhaps the activity does not appeal to you or you just want some time to yourself. Maybe you have chores or homework. If you were forced to play would you really enjoy what you were doing? Would you do your best? Yet, if you were made to join in, you might find that you had skills you never knew you had. You might even have fun.

Voting on Issues

Finally, it has been suggested that government would be more sensitive to a majority if citizens voted directly on proposed laws. This would be done by national *referenda*. Questions would be placed on ballots for voters to decide. What they decided would then become law. On issues of national importance, voters would not have to depend on the judgment of their elected officials. After all, voters do not agree with their representatives on every issue.

Critics of this proposal raise a number of questions. In an age of complicated issues and rapidly changing events, will people take the time to become informed? Will they read the newspapers, magazines, and books? Will they tune in to television and radio news and documentaries?

What if the majority vote reflects selfish interests rather than the good of the country? For example, for a hundred years after blacks had been given the right to vote, a majority of Americans refused to let them use it. They would not accept blacks as valued members of society. Black leaders and other individuals worked long and hard to convince a majority of Americans to change in their attitudes.

Not until the 1960's were many injustices against blacks remedied. During the administration of President Lyndon Johnson, Congress guaranteed equal opportunities for people to live and work where they chose, as well as to use public conveniences such as restaurants and swimming pools.

Because the majority could be wrong, the founders placed obstacles in the way of majority rule. How would you feel if student government were run mostly for the benefit of C-students? Or girls or boys, depending on their numbers?

There is yet another problem with the proposal for national referenda. What would happen if the number of voters for and against a proposed law was almost evenly divided? Sometimes, a problem is so complicated that there is no clear-cut answer.

Dr. Martin Luther King, Jr., leads civil rights marchers in 1965.

An Example

Take daylight saving time as an example. Benjamin Franklin first came up with the idea in 1784. It was designed to save energy. During World War I, the United States and several European nations decided to arrange the clock to take advantage of time when people could work without indoor lighting.

In 1986, when daylight saving time was last debated, many groups favored extending it from April to November. Many others opposed it. Parents insisted that it was safer for their children to come home from school. Businesses claimed that it reduced their electricity bills. Storekeepers said they could attract more customers. More runners could jog after work or school.

On the other hand, farmers complained that it upset animal feeding schedules. Some commuters resented having to get up in the dark to get to work. Electric companies feared they would sell less energy. Factory workers said it would be difficult to adjust to their shifts.

Those who wanted more hours of sunshine favored daylight saving time. Those who objected to resetting their clocks and schedules opposed it. This is why some states were granted the right to remain on standard time all year round. On the issue of daylight saving time, the government reached a compromise.

This example illustrates that many political issues cannot be settled by a simple yes or no. There are too many different and important points of view. That is why compromise is important. While compromise takes time, it is an important part of American politics. No one wants the majority to rule if it takes away minority rights. After all, today's minority may become tomorrow's majority. Through compromise, solutions acceptable to most Americans can be reached. Would national referenda make such compromises possible?

Daylight saving time would push this clock back an hour.

These are just some of the proposals to make the government more representative of the majority. Reformers argue that the Constitution holds us back, while conservatives claim that it helps us get ahead. Do we need to change the Constitution? You will have to decide. When you vote, listen to a political debate, discuss current events, join a political party, or even run for office, you will help determine the future of the Constitution. Will it last for another 200 years? That decision is, at least in part, up to you.

CHAPTER ACTIVITIES

Do You Know?

1. Which two of the following states have the most influence in the electoral college? (a) Montana, (b) New York, (c) Nebraska, (d) California.

2. Which of the following presidents were chosen by the House of Representatives? (a) Benjamin Harrison, (b) Grover Cleveland, (c) Thomas Jefferson, (d) John Quincy Adams.

3. If the president and Congress were elected at the same time for similar terms, which of the following would most probably happen? (a) The two branches of government would have more disagreements. (b) There would be more experienced leaders in government. (c) The government would be more likely to know what a majority of voters wanted. (d) Elections would be held more frequently.

4. Which of the following groups vote infrequently in national elections? (a) the homeless, (b) the poor, (c) the uneducated, (d) the middle-aged.

5. Which of the following groups favor daylight saving time? (a) storekeepers, (b) parents, (c) electric companies, (d) farmers.

For Discussion

1. Would you want an electoral college system to choose members of your student government? Give the reasons for your answer.

2. Why do you think people vote in elections?

3. Do you think that national referenda are a good idea? If so, what kinds of issues would you want to vote on? If not, explain why.

Research

1. List some issues on which the president and Congress have disagreed.

2. Using an almanac, find out how many eligible voters participated in the last three presidential elections.

3. Find out if your state places state and local issues on the ballot. If so, what kinds of issues are decided this way?

4. Describe some of the ways people can become active in politics.

Role Playing

Create a series of television commercials urging people to vote in elections. Then, act them out.

★

THE CONSTITUTION

❧

OF THE UNITED

❧

STATES OF AMERICA

P R E A M B L E

W<small>E, THE PEOPLE OF THE UNITED STATES,</small>
in order to form a more perfect Union, establish justice, insure domestic tranquility, provide for the common defense, promote the general welfare, and secure the blessings of liberty to ourselves and our posterity, do ordain and establish this Constitution for the United States of America.

A R T I C L E   I

Section 1. All legislative powers herein granted shall be vested in a Congress of the United States, which shall consist of a Senate and a House of Representatives.

Section 2. The House of Representatives shall be composed of members chosen every second year by the people of the several states; and the electors in each state shall have the qualifications requisite for electors of the most numerous branch of the state legislature.

No person shall be a Representative who shall not have attained the age of 25 years, and been seven years a citizen of the United States, and who shall not, when elected, be an inhabitant of that state in which he shall be chosen.

Representatives and direct taxes shall be apportioned among the several states which may be included within this Union, according to their respective numbers, which shall be determined by adding to the whole number of free persons, including those bound to service for a term of years, and excluding Indians not taxed, three fifths of all other persons. The actual enumeration shall be made within three years after the first meeting of the Congress of the United States, and within every subsequent term of ten years, in such manner as they shall by law direct. The number of Representatives shall not exceed one for every 30,000, but each state shall at have at least one Representative; and until such enumeration shall be made, the state of New Hampshire shall be entitled to choose three, Massachusetts eight, Rhode Island and Providence Plantations one, Connecticut five, New York six, New Jersey four, Pennsylvania eight, Delaware one, Maryland six, Virginia ten, North Carolina five, South Carolina five, and Georgia three.

When vacancies happen in the representation from any state, the executive authority thereof shall issue writs of election to fill such vacancies.

The House of Representatives shall choose their Speaker and other officers; and shall have the sole power of impeachment.

Section 3. The Senate of the United States shall be composed of two Senators from each state, chosen by the legislature thereof, for six years; and each Senator shall have one vote.

Immediately after they shall be assembled, in consequences of the first election, they shall be divided as equally as may be into three classes. The seats of the Senators of the first class shall be vacated at the expiration of the second year, of the second class at the expiration of the fourth year, and of the third class at the expiration of the sixth year, so that one third may be chosen every second year; and if vacancies happen by resignation, or otherwise, during the recess of the legislature of any state, the executive thereof may make temporary appointments until the next meeting of the legislature, which shall then fill such vacancies.

No person shall be a Senator who shall not have attained the age of 30 years, and been nine years a citizen of the United States, and who shall not, when elected, be an inhabitant of the state for which he shall be chosen.

The Vice-President of the United States shall be President of the Senate, but shall have no vote, unless they be equally divided.

The Senate shall choose their other officers, and also a President *Pro Tempore,* in the absence of the Vice-President, or when he shall exercise the office of President of the United States.

The Senate shall have the sole power to try all impeachments. When sitting for that purpose, they shall be on oath or affirmation. When the President of the United States is tried, the Chief Justice shall preside: and no person shall be convicted without the concurrence of two thirds of the members present.

Judgment in cases of impeachment shall not extend further than to removal from office, and disqualification to hold and enjoy any office of honor, trust, or profit, under the United States; but the party convicted shall nevertheless be liable and subject to indictment, trial, judgment, and punishment according to law.

Section 4. The times, places, and manner of holding elections for Senators and Representatives, shall be prescribed in each state by the legislature thereof; but the Congress may at any time by law make or alter such regulations, except as to the places of choosing Senators.

The Congress shall assemble at least once in every year, and such meeting shall be on the first Monday in December, unless they shall by law appoint a different day.

Section 5. Each House shall be the judge of the elections, returns, and qualifications of its own members, and a majority of each shall constitute a quorum to do business; but a smaller number may adjourn from day to day, and may be authorized to compel the attendance of absent members, in such manner, and under such penalties, as each House may provide.

Each House may determine the rules of its proceedings, punish its members for disorderly behavior, and, with the concurrence of two thirds, expel a member.

Each House shall keep a journal of its proceedings, and from time to time publish the same, excepting such parts as may, in their judgment, require secrecy; and the yeas and nays of the members of either House on any question, shall, at the desire of one fifth of those present, be entered on the journal.

Neither House, during the session of Congress, shall, without the consent of the other, adjourn for more than three days, nor to any other place than that in which the two Houses shall be sitting.

Section 6. The Senators and Representatives shall receive a compensation for their services, to be ascertained by law, and paid out of the Treasury of the United States. They shall, in all cases, except treason, felony, and breach of the peace, be privileged from arrest during their attendance at the session of their respective Houses, and in going to, and returning from, the same; and for any speech or debate in either House, they shall not be questioned in any other place.

No Senator or Representative shall, during the time for which he was elected, be appointed to any civil office under the authority of the United States, which shall have been created, or the emoluments whereof shall have been increased during such time; and no person holding any office under the United States, shall be a member of either House during his continuance in office.

Section 7. All bills for raising revenue shall originate in the House of Representatives; but the Senate may propose or concur with amendments as on other bills.

Every bill which shall have passed the House of Representatives and the Senate, shall, before it become a law, be presented to the President of the United States; if he approves he shall sign it, but if not he shall return it, with his objections, to that House in which it shall have originated, who shall enter the objections at large on their journal, and proceed to reconsider it. If after such reconsideration two thirds of that House shall agree to pass the bill, it shall be sent, together with the objections, to the other House, by which it shall likewise be reconsidered, and if approved by two thirds of that House, it shall become a law. But in all such cases the votes of both Houses shall be determined by yeas and nays, and the names of the persons voting for and against the bill shall be entered on the journal of each House respectively. If any bill shall not be returned by the President within 10 days (Sundays excepted) after it shall have been presented to him, the same shall be a law in like manner as if he had signed it, unless the Congress by their adjournment prevent its return, in which case it shall not be a law.

Every order, resolution, or vote, to which the concurrence of the Senate and House of Representatives may be necessary (except on a question of adjournment), shall be presented to the President of the United States; and before the same shall take effect, shall be approved by him, or being disapproved by him, shall be repassed by two thirds of the Senate and House of Representatives, according to the rules and limitations prescribed in the case of a bill.

Section 8. The Congress shall have power:

To lay and collect taxes, duties, imposts, and excises, to pay the debts, and provide for the common defense and general welfare of the United States; but all duties, imposts, and excises shall be uniform throughout the United States;

To borrow money on the credit of the United States;

To regulate commerce with foreign nations, and among the several states, and with the Indian tribes;

To establish a uniform rule of naturalization, and uniform laws on the subject of bankruptcies throughout the United States;

To coin money, regulate the value thereof, and of foreign coin, and fix the standard of weights and measures;

To provide for the punishment of counterfeiting the securities and current coin of the United States;

To establish post offices and post roads;

To promote the progress of science and useful arts, by securing, for limited times, to authors and inventors, the exclusive right to their respective writings and discoveries;

To constitute tribunals inferior to the Supreme Court;

To define and punish piracies and felonies committed on the high seas, and offenses against the law of nations;

To declare war, grant letters of marque and reprisal, and make rules concerning captures on land and water;

To raise and support armies; but no appropriation of money to that use shall be for a longer term than two years;

To provide and maintain a navy;

To make rules for the government and regulation of the land and naval forces;

To provide for calling forth the militia to execute the laws of the Union, suppress insurrections and repel invasions;

To provide for organizing, arming, and disciplining the militia, and for governing such part of them as may be employed in the service of the United States, reserving to the states respectively, the appointment of the officers, and the authority of training the militia according to the discipline prescribed by Congress;

To exercise exclusive legislation, in all cases whatsoever, over such district (not exceeding 10 miles square) as may, by cession of particular states, and the acceptance of Congress, become the seat of the government of the United States, and to exercise like authority over all places purchased by the consent of the legislature of the state in which the same shall be, for the erection of forts, magazines, arsenals, dockyards, and other needful buildings. And,

To make all laws which shall be necessary and proper for carrying into execution the foregoing powers, and all other powers vested by this Constitution in the government of the United States, or in any department or officer thereof.

Section 9. The migration or importation of such persons as any of the states now existing shall think proper to admit, shall not be prohibited by the Congress prior to the year 1808; but a tax or duty may be imposed on such importation, not exceeding 10 dollars for each person.

The privilege of the writ of *habeas corpus* shall not be suspended, unless when in cases of rebellion or invasion the public safety may require it.

No bill of attainder or *ex post facto* law shall be passed.

No capitation, or other direct tax, shall be laid, unless in proportion to the *census* or enumeration herein before directed to be taken.

No tax or duty shall be laid on articles exported from any state. No preference shall be given by any regulation of commerce or revenue to the ports of one state over those of another; nor shall vessels bound to, or from, one state be obliged to enter, clear, or pay duties in another.

No money shall be drawn from the treasury, but in consequence of appropriations made by law; and a regular statement and account of the receipts and expenditures of all public money shall be published from time to time.

No title of nobility shall be granted by the United States; and no person holding any office of profit or trust under them, shall, without the consent of the Congress, accept of any present, emolument, office, or title of any kind whatever, from any king, prince, or foreign state.

Section 10. No state shall enter into any treaty, alliance, or confederation; grant letters of marque and reprisal; coin money; emit bills of credit; make any thing but gold and silver coin a tender in payment of debts; pass any bill of attainder, *ex post facto* law, or law impairing the obligation of contracts, or grant any title of nobility.

No state shall, without the consent of the Congress, lay any imposts or duties on imports or exports, except what may be absolutely necessary for executing its inspection laws; and the net produce of all duties and imposts, laid by any state on imports or exports, shall be for the use of the Treasury of the United States; and all such laws shall be subject to the revision and control of the Congress. No state shall, without the consent of Congress, lay any duty of tonnage, keep troops, or ships of war, in time of peace, enter into any agreement or compact with another state, or with a foreign power, or engage in war, unless actually invaded, or in such imminent danger as will not admit of delay.

A R T I C L E I I

Section 1. The executive power shall be vested in a President of the United States of America. He shall hold his office during the term of four years, and together with the Vice-President, chosen for the same term, be elected as follows:

Each state shall appoint, in such manner as the legislature thereof may direct, a number of electors equal to the whole number of Senators and Representatives to which the state may be entitled in the Congress; but no Senator or Representative, or person holding an office of trust or profit under the United States, shall be appointed an elector.

The electors shall meet in their respective states, and vote by ballot for two persons, of whom one at least shall not be an inhabitant of the same state with themselves. And they shall make a list of all the persons voted for and of the number of votes for each; which list they shall sign and certify, and transmit sealed to the seat of the government of the United States, directed to the President of the Senate. The President of the Senate shall, in the presence of the Senate and House of Representatives, open all the certificates, and the votes shall then be counted. The person having the greatest number of votes shall be the President, if such number be a majority of the whole number of electors appointed; and if there be more than one who have such majority, and have an equal number of votes, then the House of Representatives shall immediately choose by ballot one of them for President; and if no person have a majority, then from the five highest on the list the said House shall in like manner choose the President. But in choosing the President, the votes shall be taken by states, the representation from each state having one vote; a quorum for this purpose shall consist of a member or members from two thirds of the states, and a majority of all the states shall be necessary to a choice. In every case, after the choice of the President, the person having the greatest number of votes of the electors shall be the Vice-President. But if there should remain two or more who have equal votes, the Senate shall choose from them by ballot the Vice-President.

The Congress may determine the time of choosing the electors, and the day on which they shall give their votes; which day shall be the same throughout the United States.

No person except a natural-born citizen, or a citizen of the United States, at the time of the adoption of this Constitution, shall be eligible to the office of President; neither shall any person be eligible to that office who shall not have attained the age of 35 years, and been 14 years a resident within the United States.

In case of the removal of the President from office, or of his death, resignation, or inability to discharge the powers and duties of the said office, the same shall devolve on the Vice-President, and the Congress may by law provide for the case of removal, death, resignation, or inability, both of the President and Vice-President, declaring what officer shall then act as President, and such officer shall act accordingly until the disability be removed, or a President shall be elected.

The President shall at stated times receive for his services a compensation, which shall neither be increased nor diminished during the period for which he shall have been elected, and he shall not receive within that period any other emolument from the United States or any of them.

Before he enter on the execution of his office, he shall take the following oath or affirmation:

"I do solemnly swear (or affirm) that I will faithfully execute the office of President of the United States, and will, to the best of my ability, preserve, protect, and defend the Constitution of the United States."

Section 2. The President shall be Commander-in-Chief of the Army and Navy of the United States, and of the militia of the several states, when called into the actual service of the United States; he may require the opinion, in writing, of the principal officer in each of the executive departments, upon any subject relating to the duties of their respective offices, and he shall have power to grant reprieves and pardons for offenses against the United States, except in cases of impeachment.

He shall have power, by and with the advice and consent of the Senate, to make treaties, provided two thirds of the Senators present concur; and he shall nominate, and by and with the advice and consent of the Senate, shall appoint ambassadors, other public ministers and consuls, judges of the Supreme Court, and all other officers of the United States, whose appointments are not herein otherwise provided for, and which shall be established by law. But the Congress may by law vest the appointment of such inferior officers, as they think proper, in the President alone, in the courts of law, or in the heads of departments.

The President shall have power to fill up all vacancies that may happen during the recess of the Senate, by granting commissions which shall expire at the end of their next session.

Section 3. He shall, from time to time, give to the Congress information of the state of the Union, and recommend to their consideration such measures as he shall judge necessary and expedient. He may on extraordinary occasions, convene both Houses, or either of them; and in case of disagreement between them, with respect to the time of adjournment, he may adjourn them to such time as he shall think proper. He shall receive ambassadors and other public ministers. He shall take care that the laws be faithfully executed; and shall commission all the officers of the United States.

Section 4. The President, Vice-President, and all civil officers of the United States, shall be removed from office on impeachment for, and conviction of, treason, bribery, or other high crimes and misdemeanors.

A R T I C L E   I   I   I

Section 1. The judicial power of the United States shall be vested in one Supreme Court, and in such inferior courts as the Congress may, from time to time, ordain and establish. The judges, both of the Supreme and inferior courts, shall hold their offices during good behavior; and shall, at stated times, receive for their services, a compensation, which shall not be diminished during their continuance in office.

Section 2. The judicial power shall extend to all cases, in law and equity, arising under this Constitution, the laws of the United States, and treaties made, or which shall be made, under their authority; to all cases affecting ambassadors, other public ministers, and consuls; to all cases of admiralty and maritime jurisdiction; to controversies to which the United States shall be a party; to controversies between two or more states, between a state and citizens of another state, between citizens of different states, between citizens of the same state claiming lands under grants of different states, and between a state, or the citizens thereof, and foreign states, citizens, or subjects.

In all cases affecting ambassadors, other public ministers and consuls, and those in which a state shall be party, the Supreme Court shall have original jurisdiction. In all the other cases before mentioned, the Supreme Court shall have appellate jurisdiction, both as to law and fact, with such exceptions, and under such regulations, as the Congress shall make.

The trial of all crimes, except in cases of impeachment, shall be by jury; and such trial shall be held in the state where the said crimes shall have been committed; but when not committed within any state, the trial shall be at such place or places as the Congress may by law have directed.

Section 3. Treason against the United States, shall consist only in levying war against them, or in adhering to their enemies, giving them aid and comfort. No person shall be convicted of treason unless on the testimony of two witnesses to the same overt act, or on confession in open court.

The Congress shall have power to declare the punishment of treason, but no attainder of treason shall work corruption of blood, or forfeiture, except during the life of the person attainted.

A   R   T   I   C   L   E   I   V

Section 1. Full faith and credit shall be given in each state to the public acts, records, and judicial proceedings of every other state. And the Congress may by general laws prescribe the manner in which such acts, records, and proceedings shall be proved, and the effect thereof.

Section 2. The citizens of each state shall be entitled to all privileges and immunities of citizens in the several states.

A person charged in any state with treason, felony, or other crimes, who shall flee from justice, and be found in another state, shall, on demand of the executive authority of the state from which he fled, be delivered up to be removed to the state having jurisdiction of the crime.

No person held to service or labor in one state, under the laws thereof, escaping into another, shall, in consequence of any laws or regulation therein, be discharged from such service or labor, but shall be delivered up on claim of the party to whom such service or labor may be due.

Section 3. New states may be admitted by the Congress into this Union; but no new state shall be formed or erected within the jurisdiction of any other state; nor any state be formed by the junction of two or more states or parts of states, without the consent of the legislatures of the states concerned, as well as of the Congress.

The Congress shall have power to dispose of and make all needful rules and regulations respecting the territory or other property belonging to the United States; and nothing in this Constitution shall be so construed as to prejudice any claims of the United States, or of any particular state.

Section 4. The United States shall guarantee to every state in this Union a republican form of government, and shall protect each of them against invasion; and on application of the legislature, or of the executive (when the legislature cannot be convened), against domestic violence.

A R T I C L E V

The Congress, whenever two thirds of both Houses shall deem it necessary, shall propose amendments to this Constitution, or, on the application of the legislatures of two thirds of the several states, shall call a convention for proposing amendments, which, in either case, shall be valid to all intents and purposes, as part of this Constitution, when ratified by the legislatures of three fourths of the several states, or by conventions in three fourths thereof, as the one or the other mode of ratification may be proposed by the Congress; provided that no amendment, which may be made prior to the year 1808, shall in any manner affect the first and fourth clauses in the ninth section of the first article; and that no state, without its consent, shall be deprived of its equal suffrage in the Senate.

A R T I C L E V I

All debts contracted, and engagements entered into, before the adoption of this Constitution, shall be as valid against the United States, under this Constitution, as under the Confederation.

This Constitution, and the laws of the United States which shall be made in pursuance thereof, and all treaties made, or which shall be made, under the authority of the United States, shall be the supreme law of the land; and the judges, in every state, shall be bound thereby, anything in the constitution or laws of any state to the contrary notwithstanding.

The Senators and Representatives before mentioned, and the members of the several state legislatures, and all executive and judicial officers, both of the United States and of the several states, shall be bound, by oath or affirmation, to support this Constitution; but no religious test shall ever be required as a qualification to any office or public trust under the United States.

ARTICLE VII

The ratification of the conventions of nine states shall be sufficient for the establishment of this Constitution between the states so ratifying the same.

AMENDMENTS

(The first ten amendments, adopted in 1791, are called the Bill of Rights.)

AMENDMENT I. Congress shall make no law respecting an establishment of religion, or prohibiting the free exercise thereof; or abridging the freedom of speech, or of the press, or the right of the people peaceably to assemble, and to petition the government for a redress of grievances.

AMENDMENT II. A well regulated militia being necessary to the security of a free state, the right of the people to keep and bear arms shall not be infringed.

AMENDMENT III. No soldier shall, in time of peace, be quartered in any house without the consent of the owner; nor in time of war, but in a manner to be prescribed by law.

AMENDMENT IV. The right of the people to be secure in their persons, houses, papers, and effects, against unreasonable searches and seizures, shall not be violated; and no warrants shall issue, but upon probable cause, supported by oath or affirmation, and particularly describing the place to be searched, and the persons and things to be seized.

AMENDMENT V. No person shall be held to answer for a capital or otherwise infamous crime, unless on a presentment or indictment of a grand jury, except in cases arising in the land or naval forces, or in the militia, when in actual service, in time of war or public danger; nor shall any person be subject for the same offenses to be twice put in jeopardy of life or limb; nor shall be compelled, in any criminal case, to be a witness against himself; nor shall be deprived of life, liberty, or property, without due process of law; nor shall private property be taken for public use without just compensation.

AMENDMENT VI. In all criminal prosecutions the accused shall enjoy the right to a speedy and public trial, by an impartial jury of the state and district wherein the crime shall have been committed, which district shall have been previously ascertained by law, and to be informed of the nature and cause of the accusation; to be confronted with the witnesses against him; to have compulsory process for obtaining witnesses in his favor; and to have the assist of counsel in his defense.

AMENDMENT VII. In suits at common law, where the value in controversy shall exceed 20 dollars, the right of trial by jury shall be preserved; and no fact tried by a jury shall be otherwise re-examined in any court of the United States than according to the rules of the common law.

AMENDMENT VIII. Excessive bail shall not be required, nor excessive fines imposed, nor cruel and unusual punishments inflicted.

AMENDMENT IX. The enumeration in the Constitution of certain rights shall not be construed to deny or disparage others retained by the people.

AMENDMENT X. The powers not delegated to the United States by the Constitution, nor prohibited by it to the states, are reserved to the states respectively or to the people.

AMENDMENT XI (1798). The judicial power of the United States shall not be construed to extend to any suit in law or equity, commenced or prosecuted against one of the United States by citizens of any state, or by citizens or subjects of any foreign state.

AMENDMENT XII (1804). The electors shall meet in their respective states, and vote by ballot for President and Vice-President, one of whom, at least, shall not be an inhabitant of the same state with themselves; they shall name in their ballots the person voted for as President, and in distinct ballots the person voted for as Vice-President; and they shall make distinct lists of all persons voted for as President, and of all persons voted for as Vice-President, and of the number of votes for each, which list they shall sign and certify, and transmit, sealed, to the seat of the government of the United States, directed to the President of the Senate; the President of the Senate shall, in the presence of the Senate and House of Representatives, open all the certificates, and the votes shall then be counted. The person having the greatest number of votes for President shall be the President, if such number be a majority of the whole number of electors appointed; and if no person have such majority, then from the persons having the highest numbers, not exceeding three, on the list of those voted for as President, the House of Representatives shall choose immediately, by ballot, the President. But in choosing the President, the votes shall be taken by states, the representation from each state having one vote; a quorum for this purpose shall consist of a member or members from two thirds of the states, and a majority of all the states shall be necessary to a choice. And if the House of Representatives shall not choose a President whenever the right of choice shall devolve upon them, before the fourth day of March next following, then the Vice-President shall act as President, as in the case of the death or other constitutional disability of the President.

The person having the greatest number of votes as Vice-President shall be the Vice-President, if such number be a majority of the whole number of electors appointed; and if no person have a majority, then from the two highest numbers on the list the Senate shall choose the Vice-President. A quorum for the purpose shall consist of two thirds of the whole number of Senators, and a majority of the whole number shall be necessary to a choice.

But no person constitutionally ineligible to the office of President shall be eligible to that of Vice-President of the United States.

AMENDMENT XIII (1865). *Section 1.* Neither slavery nor involuntary servitude, except as punishment for a crime whereof the party shall have been duly convicted, shall exist within the United States, or any place subject to their jurisdiction.

Section 2. Congress shall have power to enforce this article by appropriate legislation.

AMENDMENT XIV (1868). *Section 1.* All persons born or naturalized in the United States, and subject to the jurisdiction thereof, are citizens of the United States and of the state wherein they reside. No state shall make or enforce any law which shall abridge the privileges or immunities of citizens of the United States; nor shall any state deprive any person of life, liberty, or property, without due process of law, nor deny to any person within its jurisdiction the equal protection of the laws.

Section 2. Representatives shall be apportioned among the several states according to their respective numbers, counting the whole number of persons in each state, excluding Indians not taxed. But when the right to vote at any election for the choice of electors for President and Vice-President of the United States, representatives in Congress, the executive and judicial officers of a state, or the members of the legislature thereof, is denied to any of the male inhabitants of such state, being 21 years of age, and citizens of the United States, or in anyway abridged, except for participation in rebellion or other crime, the basis of representation therein shall be reduced in the proportion which the number of such male citizens shall bear to the whole number of male citizens 21 years of age in such state.

Section 3. No person shall be a Senator or Representative in Congress, or elector of President and Vice-President, or hold any office, civil or military, under the United States, or under any state, who, having previously taken an oath, as a member of Congress, or as an officer of the United States, or as a member of any state legislature, or as an executive or judicial officer of any state, to support the Constitution of the United States, shall have engaged in insurrection or rebellion against the same, or given aid or comfort to the enemies thereof. But Congress may, by a vote of two thirds of each house, remove such disability.

Section 4. The validity of the public debt of the United States, authorized by law, including debts incurred for payment of pensions and bounties for services in supressing insurrection or rebellion, shall not be questioned. But neither the United States nor any state shall assume or pay any debt or obligation incurred in aid of insurrection or rebellion against the United States, or any claim for the loss or emancipation of any slave; but all such debts, obligations, and claims shall be held illegal and void.

Section 5. The Congress shall have power to enforce, by appropriate legislation, the provisions of this article.

AMENDMENT XV (1870). *Section 1.* The right of citizens of the United States to vote shall not be denied or abridged by the United States or by any state on account of race, color or previous condition of servitude.

Section 2. The Congress shall have power to enforce this article by appropriate legislation.

AMENDMENT XVI (1913). The Congress shall have power to lay and collect taxes on incomes, from whatever source derived, without apportionment among the several states, and without regard to any census or enumeration.

AMENDMENT XVII (1913). The Senate of the United States shall be composed of two Senators from each state, elected by the people thereof, for six years; and each Senator shall have one vote. The electors in each state shall have the qualifications requisite for electors of the most numerous branch of the state legislatures.

When vacancies happen in the representation of any state in the Senate, the executive authority of such state shall issue writs of election to fill such vacancies: *Provided,* That the legislature of any state may empower the executive thereof to make temporary appointments until the people fill the vacancies by election as the legislature may direct.

This amendment shall not be so construed as to effect the election or term of any Senator chosen before it becomes valid as part of the Constitution.

AMENDMENT XVIII (1919). *Section 1.* After one year from the ratification of this article the manufacture, sale, or transportation of intoxicating liquors within, the importation thereof into, or the exportation thereof from the United States and all territory subject to the jurisdiction thereof for beverage purposes is hereby prohibited.

Section 2. The Congress and the several states shall have concurrent power to enforce this article by appropriate legislation.

Section 3. This article shall be inoperative unless it shall have been ratified as an amendment to the Constitution by the legislatures of the several states, as provided in the Constitution, within seven years from the date of the submission hereof to the states by the Congress.

AMENDMENT XIX (1920). The right of citizens of the United States to vote shall not be denied or abridged by the United States or by any state on account of sex.

Congress shall have power to enforce this article by appropriate legislation.

AMENDMENT XX (1933). *Section 1.* The terms of the President and Vice-President shall end at noon on the 20th day of January, and the terms of Senators and Representatives at noon on the 3rd day of January, of the years in which such terms would have ended if this article had not been ratified; and the terms of their successors shall then begin.

Section 2. The Congress shall assemble at least once in every year, and such meeting shall begin at noon on the 3rd day of January, unless they shall by law appoint a different day.

Section 3. If, at the time fixed for the beginning of the term of the President, the President-elect shall have died, the Vice-President-elect shall become President. If a President shall not have been chosen before the time fixed for the beginning of his term, or if the President-elect shall have failed to qualify, then the Vice-President elect shall act as President until a President shall have qualified; and the Congress may by law provide for the case wherein neither a President-elect nor a Vice-President-elect shall have qualified, declaring who shall then act as President, or the manner in which one who is to act shall be selected, and such person shall act accordingly until a President or Vice-President shall have qualified.

Section 4. The Congress may by law provide for the case of the death of any of the persons from whom the House of Representatives may choose a President whenever the right of choice shall have devolved upon them, and for the case of the death of any of the persons from whom the Senate may choose a Vice-President whenever the right of choice shall have devolved upon them.

Section 5. Sections 1 and 2 shall take affect on the 15th day of October following the ratification of this article.

Section 6. This article shall be inoperative unless it shall have been ratified as an amendment to the Constitution by the legislatures of three fourths of the several states within seven years from the date of its submission.

AMENDMENT XXI (1933). *Section 1.* The 18th article of amendment to the Constitution of the United States is hereby repealed.

Section 2. The transportation or importation into any state, territory, or possession of the United States for delivery or use therein of intoxicating liquors, in violation of the laws thereof, is hereby prohibited.

Section 3. This article shall be inoperative unless it shall have been ratified as an amendment to the Constitution by conventions in the several states, as provided in the Constitution, within seven years from the date of the submission hereof to the states by the Congress.

AMENDMENT XXII (1951). No person shall be elected to the office of the President more than twice, and no person who has held the office of President, or acted as President, for more than two years of a term to which some other person was elected President shall be elected to the office of the President more than once. But this article shall not apply to any person holding the office of President when this article was proposed by the Congress, and shall not prevent any person who may be holding the office of President, or acting as President, during the term within which this article becomes operative from holding the office of President or acting as President during the remainder of such term.

AMENDMENT XXIII (1961). *Section 1.* The district constituting the seat of government of the United States shall appoint in such a manner as the Congress may direct: A number of electors of President and Vice-President equal to the whole number of Senators and Representatives in Congress to which the district would be entitled if it were a state, but in no event more than the least populous state; they shall be in addition to those appointed by the states, but they shall be considered, for the purposes of the election of the President and Vice-President, to be electors appointed by a state; and they shall meet in the district and perform such duties as provided by the 12th article of amendment.

Section 2. The Congress shall have power to enforce this article by appropriate legislation.

AMENDMENT XXIV (1964). *Section 1.* The right of citizens of the United States to vote in any primary or other election for President or Vice-President, for electors for President or Vice-President, or for Senator or Representatives in Congress, shall not be denied or abridged by the United States or any state by reason of failure to pay any poll tax or other tax.

Section 2. The Congress shall have the power to enforce this article by appropriate legislation.

AMENDMENT XXV (1967). *Section 1.* In case of the removal of the President from office or his death or resignation, the Vice-President shall become President.

Section 2. Whenever there is a vacancy in the office of the Vice-President, the President shall nominate a Vice-President who shall take office upon confirmation by a majority vote of both houses of Congress.

Section 3. Whenever the President transmits to the President *Pro Tempore* of the Senate and the Speaker of the House of Representatives his written declaration that he is unable to discharge the powers and duties of his office, and until he transmits to them a written declaration to the contrary, such powers and duties shall be discharged by the Vice-President as Acting President.

Section 4. Whenever the Vice-President and a majority of either the principal officers of the executive departments or of such other body as Congress may by law provide, transmit to the President *Pro Tempore* of the Senate and the Speaker of the House of Representatives their written declaration that the President is unable to discharge the powers and duties of his office, the Vice-President shall immediately assume the powers and duties of the office as Acting President.

Thereafter, when the President transmits to the President *Pro Tempore* of the Senate and the Speaker of the House of Representatives his written declaration that no inability exists, he shall resume the powers and duties of his office unless the Vice-President and a majority of either the principal officers of the executive departments or of such other body as Congress may by law provide, transmit within four days to the President *Pro Tempore* of the Senate and the Speaker of the House of Representatives their written declaration that the President is unable to discharge the powers and duties of his office. Thereupon Congress shall decide the issue, assembling within 48 hours for that purpose if not in session. If the Congress, within 21 days after receipt of the latter written declaration, or, if Congress is not in session, within 21 days after Congress is required to assemble, determines by two-thirds vote of both houses that the President is unable to discharge the powers and duties of his office, the Vice-President shall continue to discharge the same as Acting President; otherwise, the President shall resume the powers and duties of his office.

AMENDMENT XXVI (1971). *Section 1.* The right of citizens of the United States, who are 18 years of age or older, to vote shall not be denied or abridged by the United States or any state on account of age.

Section 2. The Congress shall have power to enforce this article by appropriate legislation.

GLOSSARY

amendments. Additions or changes to laws or the Constitution.

Antifederalists. A group of patriots who refused to approve the new Constitution. They felt that the federal government would be undemocratic and far too powerful. They demanded that a bill of rights be added to the Constitution.

Articles of Confederation. An agreement signed by the 13 original colonies after the American Revolution. It set up an ineffective association of states which was the government of the United States from 1781 to 1789.

bail. Money given as a pledge that permits a person accused of a crime to leave jail before the trial is held. If the person fails to appear for the trial, the money is forfeited.

bankruptcy. Inability to pay debts.

bill of attainder. Laws which punish specific individuals or groups without benefit of a trial.

bill of rights. List of specific freedoms that governments cannot threaten or take away. The first 10 amendments to the Constitution are the American Bill of Rights.

cabinet. Heads of government departments and other officials in the executive branch of government who meet regularly to help carry out presidential duties.

caucus. A meeting of a small group of people. The first American political parties used caucuses to select candidates.

checks and balances. The idea that each of the three branches of the American government plays a part in the work of the others. Checks and balances require the competing branches to cooperate and compromise in order to govern.

consent. Approval, agreement, or permission.

constitution. A framework or organization of parts. Constitutions set up the structures of government.

constitutionalism. The idea that governments must be limited by law and prevented from using their powers to deprive their citizens of liberty.

corruption of the blood and forfeiture. Treating the innocent families and descendants of persons convicted of treason as guilty of disloyalty and taking away their property.

delegates. People chosen to be representatives or spokespersons for others.

domestic insurrection. Riots, rebellions, and other uprisings against established authority.

due process of law. A set of legal procedures which guarantees citizens a fair trial. The Fifth and 14th Amendments to the Constitution require the national and state governments to follow these procedures.

elastic clause. Gives Congress the power to "make all laws which shall be necessary and proper" to carry out its constitutional responsibilities. It allows Congress to broaden definitions of what it may do.

electoral college system. The method the Constitution prescribes to elect the president and vice-president.

electorate. The voters in an election.

electors. Special delegates chosen to vote for the president and vice-president. Collectively, they form the electoral college.

eminent domain. The government's power to take away private property for a public purpose. The Constitution requires the government to pay citizens when it exercises this right.

ex post facto laws. Legislation that punishes people for acts that were not considered criminal at the time they were committed.

Executive Office of the President. Created in 1939 to help the president carry out the responsibilities of office. It is made up of organizations such as the National Security Council, which advises the president on ways to protect the United States from its enemies, and the Council of Economic Advisors, which makes recommendations about how to keep the economy healthy.

executive powers. The authority to put laws into effect, to appoint officials, and to engage in international relations. In the United States, executive power belongs primarily to the president.

exports. Goods produced for sale in other countries.

express powers. Authority which the Constitution specifically gives to one branch of government. For example, Congress's right to set standard weights and measures is an express power.

extradition. The constitutional requirement that a state return escaped criminals who seek to avoid trial or imprisonment by fleeing to another state.

federalism. A system of ruling which divides power between a national government and state governments.

Federalists. Originally, a group of men who helped win acceptance for the Constitution. The Federalists became one of the first political parties in the United States. They supported a strong national government and policies that would help business and commercial interests.

fines. Money paid as punishment for a crime.

full faith and credit. The constitutional obligation that states accept as legal the public documents and records of other states.

fundamental law. Describes the ideals of a society and lays the foundation for its institutions. It creates basic governmental structures. In the United States, the Constitution is regarded as fundamental law.

grand jury. A group of citizens who determine whether there is enough evidence to try a person accused of a serious crime.

Great Depression. The collapse of the American economy that occurred during the 1930's. Unemployment was widespread, many businesses closed, farms lay idle, and prices fell.

Gross National Product. The value of all goods and services produced in the United States.

impeachment. The first step in removing the president or other high government officials from office as prescribed by the Constitution.

implied powers. The ability of Congress to do what is necessary and proper to carry out its specific duties. The Constitution grants Congress implied powers in the elastic clause.

independent agencies. Organizations within the executive branch that are not attached to any government departments. Created by Congress, these agencies have legislative, executive, and judicial powers. One example is the National Aeronautics and Space Administration (NASA).

interstate. Among states, crossing state boundaries. An example of an interstate activity is a truck transporting produce from Los Angeles to Chicago.

intrastate. Within one state. An example of an intrastate activity is a truck hauling crates from Raleigh, North Carolina, to Charlotte, North Carolina.

judicial power. The authority to hold trials, to rule on appeals from those trials, to run the court system, and to interpret what the laws mean. In the United States, judicial power is exercised by judges in state and national courts.

judicial review. The power to decide whether the acts of states, the Congress, or the president are permitted by the Constitution. Judicial review is not mentioned in the Constitution, but the Supreme Court claimed the final authority to make such judgments.

lame ducks. Officials who have been defeated for reelection and are serving the remainder of their terms of office. A president in the second term of office can also be considered a lame duck because running for reelection is prohibited by the 22nd Amendment.

League of Nations. An international organization that came into existence after World War I and lasted until World War II. It had a council and an assembly in which nations could meet and discuss problems of mutual interest.

legislative power. The authority to make laws. In the United States, responsibility for making national laws is given to the Congress as representatives of the people.

letters of marque and reprisal. Permission given to private trading ships to seize hostile vessels and their cargoes without being accused of piracy.

loose constructionists. People who believe that the words of the Constitution should be interpreted very broadly or flexibly.

naturalization. The process which allows immigrants to the United States to become citizens. Congress has set requirements for naturalization which include five years residence in the United States, an understanding of the English language, and a knowledge of American history and government.

nominating convention. A meeting of delegates for the purpose of choosing candidates for political office and deciding what positions the party will take on the outstanding issues of the day. Delegates from the state Democratic and Republican parties each hold conventions every four years to select presidential and vice-presidential candidates. The Constitution does not say anything about nominating conventions.

overriding a veto. A means by which the Congress can pass a law even though the president has rejected it. Overriding a veto requires a two-thirds vote in the House and the Senate.

perjury. Lying under oath. Perjury is punishable by law.

political parties. Organizations that select candidates to run for office and conduct campaigns to get their candidates elected. Parties also take positions on issues which their candidates are expected to support.

poll tax. A fee citizens had to pay in some states in order to vote in elections. The 24th Amendment prohibited the use of poll taxes in national elections.

popular vote. Votes cast directly by the people.

preamble. An introductory statement of purpose and goals.

primaries. Special elections to choose a political party's candidates for office.

privileges and immunities. The constitutional requirement that states treat citizens of other states the way they treat their own citizens. There are exceptions to this rule. For example, out-of-state visitors are not entitled to vote in state elections.

ratify. To approve or accept. The Constitution had to be ratified by nine states before it could be put into effect.

referenda. Issues put on the ballot for voters to decide. For example, in California, voters were asked to accept or reject Proposition 13 which limited the amount of property taxes they would have to pay.

repeal. To cancel, take back, or withdraw. The 18th Amendment to the Constitution banning the sale of alcoholic beverages was repealed by the 21st Amendment.

representative democracy. A form of government in which people have the right to regularly elect individuals to be their spokespersons, to make laws, and carry them out.

republican form of government. A system run by officials elected by the people. After the American Revolution, the United States became a republic.

reserve powers. Authority which has been set aside for future use. According to the 10th Amendment, the states have reserve powers.

secretaries. The title given to the heads of departments in the executive branch of government. The head of the Department of State is known as the secretary of state.

self-incrimination. Being forced to testify against yourself. The Fifth Amendment prohibits the government from forcing citizens to make confessions which could be used against them in a court of law.

separation of powers. The idea of dividing or setting apart the functions of government and distributing them among several branches.

strict constructionists. People who believe that the words of the Constitution should be interpreted very narrowly.

treason. The act of waging war against the United States or siding with America's enemies and helping them. The Constitution defines treason very precisely to prevent it from being used to punish political opponents or stifle disagreements.

veto. Presidential rejection of a bill Congress has passed. According to the Constitution, the president can refuse to sign a bill into law and return it to Congress with his objections.

White House Staff. A group of assistants who help the president. Members of the White House Staff include such officials as a press secretary, a national security affairs advisor, and a lawyer. They offer advice.

writ of habeas corpus. An order which explains to a judge why law enforcement officials are holding an individual in custody. The Constitution's requirement for a writ of habeas corpus protects suspects from being kept in jail without a stated cause.

I N D E X